www.wadsworth.com

www.wadsworth.com is the World Wide Web site for Thomson Wadsworth and is your direct source to dozens of online resources.

At *www.wadsworth.com* you can find out about supplements, demonstration software, and student resources. You can also send email to many of our authors and preview new publications and exciting new technologies.

www.wadsworth.com
Changing the way the world learns®

Decision Cases for Generalist Social Work Practice

Decision Cases for Generalist Social Work Practice

Thinking Like a Social Worker

Edited by

T. LAINE SCALES
Baylor University

TERRY A. WOLFER
University of South Carolina

THOMSON

BROOKS/COLE

Australia • Brazil • Canada • Mexico • Singapore • Spain
United Kingdom • United States

THOMSON

TM

BROOKS/COLE

Decision Cases for Generalist Social Work Practice: Thinking Like a Social Worker
T. Laine Scales and Terry A. Wolfer

Publisher/Executive Editor: *Lisa Gebo*
Assistant Editor: *Monica Arvin*
Editorial Assistant: *Sheila Walsh*
Technology Project Manager: *Barry Connolly*
Marketing Manager: *Caroline Concilla*
Marketing Assistant: *Rebecca Weisman*
Advertising Project Manager: *Tami Strang*
Project Manager, Editorial Production: *Megan E. Hansen*

Art Director: *Vernon Boes*
Print Buyer: *Lisa Claudeanos*
Permissions Editor: *Kiely Sisk*
Production Service: *Sara Dovre Wudali, Buuji, Inc.*
Copy Editor: *Cheryl Hauser*
Cover Designer: *Andy Norris*
Compositor: *International Typesetting and Composition*
Printer: *Malloy Incorporated*

For more information about our products, contact us at:
Thomson Learning Academic Resource Center
1-800-423-0563

For permission to use material from this text or product, submit a request online at
http://www.thomsonrights.com.
Any additional questions about permissions can be submitted by email to
thomsonrights@thomson.com.

Library of Congress Control Number: 2005925201

ISBN 0-534-52194-0

Thomson Higher Education
10 Davis Drive
Belmont, CA 94002-3098
USA

Asia (including India)
Thomson Learning
5 Shenton Way
#01-01 UIC Building
Singapore 068808

Australia/New Zealand
Thomson Learning Australia
102 Dodds Street
Southbank, Victoria 3006
Australia

Canada
Thomson Nelson
1120 Birchmount Road
Toronto, Ontario M1K 5G4
Canada

UK/Europe/Middle East/Africa
Thomson Learning
High Holborn House
50/51 Bedford Row
London WC1R 4LR
United Kingdom

Latin America
Thomson Learning
Seneca, 53
Colonia Polanco
11560 Mexico
D.F. Mexico

Spain (including Portugal)
Thomson Paraninfo
Calle Magallanes, 25
28015 Madrid, Spain

To Glenn Blalock and Regina Yutzy-Wolfer for their constant encouragement, support, and love.

Contents

PREFACE   **XI**

ABOUT THE EDITORS   **XV**

CASE AUTHOR BIOGRAPHIES   **XVII**

PART I ABOUT DECISION CASES   1

CHAPTER 1 AN INTRODUCTION TO DECISION CASES AND CASE METHOD LEARNING   3

What Is Your Experience with Cases?   4

Cases in Social Work Education   5

Distinguishing Decision Cases from Other Types   6

Outcomes of Decision Case Learning   8

Case Method Teaching   11

The Cases   11

Where these Cases Came from, and How They Were Written   12

Reading the Cases   14

References   14

CHAPTER 2 TIPS FOR LEARNING FROM DECISION CASES   17

Reading the Case   17

Digging into the Case Situation: Develop Your "Awareness"   18

Develop Empathic Understanding   19

Defining or Formulating the Problem   19

Analysis: Identifying the Key Issues and How They Relate   20

Prepare to Participate: Take a Stand   21

Things to Avoid while Preparing   21

Actively Support Your Conclusions in the Discussion, But Stay Open to Emerging Insights   22

Listen Carefully   22

Making Contributions   23

Things to Avoid in Case Discussions   23

Trust the Process   24

Focus on Here-and-Now Process, and Results Will Follow   24

Maintain Perspective   25

Finally, Focus on Long-Term Outcomes   25

References   25

PART II CASES   27

CASE 1   THREAT TO SOCIETY?   29

CASE 2   TWICE A VICTIM. . . . IN ENGLISH, PLEASE   39

CASE 3   I CAN'T FIND HER!   47

CASE 4   I NEED TO ADVOCATE FOR MY CLIENT!   55

CASE 5   CARLA FIGHTS THE SYSTEM   67

CASE 6   THIS COULD GET MESSY   75

CASE 7   IN NEED OF SUPPORT   83

CASE 8   THE DISCHARGE DILEMMA   95

CASE 9   THE RIDGE   105

CASE 10 IF ONLY . . . !   113

CASE 11 FINDING OUR WAY   123

CASE 12 IN HER BEST INTEREST   137

Preface

As social work educators, we face the challenge of bridging the perennial gap between theory and practice in our classrooms. When we talk with students and practitioners, we see how traditional methods of classroom instruction may not adequately prepare students for the complexities, messiness, and ambiguities of actual social work practice. In the past five years we have been interested in finding ways to bring real social work experiences into the classroom setting as instructional tools. Since we discovered case discussion and the impact it can have on a social worker's development, we have worked on several case collections for classroom use.

We are fortunate that some of our colleagues in our respective universities have "caught" our deep enthusiasm for this method of teaching. Once teachers and students experience a dynamic classroom where people come alive dissecting a messy social work problem, and once they feel the satisfaction of using critical thinking skills and formulating potential responses, they begin to see why we appreciate this teaching method.

In 1999, a few social work faculty members at Baylor University began experimenting with decision cases when we were particularly eager to introduce our students to practice situations involving a variety of religious and spiritual traditions. Faculty members, including field instructors, from Baylor joined Laine, Terry, and faculty from other universities to develop cases collaboratively, prepare written teaching notes, and try them out with our students.

Meanwhile, at the University of South Carolina, Terry and his colleagues were developing a case-based MSW capstone course. Thus far, more than 1,000 MSW students at USC's College of Social Work have benefited from the capstone course before heading off to practice in South Carolina and across the nation. Though tales of the course still create anxiety for some students, empirical evaluation, and a growing group of graduates, field instructors, and faculty members attest to its value.

In 2003, Terry launched *Decision Cases for Advanced Social Work Practice,* a collection of cases drawn from USC's MSW capstone course, and invited Laine to co-edit that collection. Soon we recognized the need for a similar collection of decision cases for BSW-level students and foundation-level MSW students preparing for generalist practice. As a result, we assembled a group of baccalaureate social work educators to identify case reporters willing to share cases that would be instructive for students learning to "think like social workers" in generalist practice.

Although these cases have been disguised to protect individuals and organizations, we avoided making changes (i.e., gender, ethnicity, region) that would alter case dynamics. In the interest of case fidelity, we retained approximate dates and numerous other details that experienced practitioners know make a difference when assessing a situation.

These decision cases come from many contexts of practice and involve social workers in diverse practice roles. As students enter generalist practice with individuals, families, groups, communities, and organizations, we think is it essential for them to understand the social policies and administrative contexts that will inevitably and profoundly influence their work. Further, we think it is important for social work students to understand the perspectives of their supervisors and agency administrators, including the effects of interpersonal dynamics at those levels. In all these settings, social workers repeatedly encounter novel and surprising situations. We share a vision for social work that strives to hold our profession's differences in tension, and we see these differences as strengths.

In addition to what students may learn about unfamiliar social work settings and interventions, these cases provide opportunity for practicing the fundamental skills of formulating and analyzing problems, and deciding how to respond. The cases depict complex and challenging practice situations. We do not offer the cases as examples of either good or poor practice but rather as puzzles to resolve together.

Many people have assisted us in learning case method teaching and case writing and helped us introduce the method to our colleagues and students.

I (Laine) would like to thank my friend Terry, with whom I have enjoyed collaborating on so many different kinds of professional projects, for initially introducing me to case method teaching six years ago and for suggesting that we collaborate on this project. I also am indebted to my colleagues in the Baylor University School of Social Work for their willingness to embrace case method teaching, to pilot our cases, and to create new cases to stimulate our students. Finally, my greatest appreciation and love goes to my husband, Glenn Blalock, an extraordinary teacher and writer and the one who encourages me best to keep working at new ways of teaching.

I (Terry) would like to thank Michael Welsh who first introduced me to case method teaching and who remains a good friend, mentor, and collaborator on case method teaching, and who also introduced me to the North American Case Research Association. I thank Deans Raymond and Ginsberg for continuing support of the capstone course, faculty development, and case writing. I also thank colleagues Rita Rhodes and Karen Gray for their committed leadership of the capstone faculty group, and Vicki Runnion for collaboration on another case project. In compiling this case collection, I am grateful to Laine Scales, a good friend and colleague who shared editorial responsibilities for this and the companion case collection for advanced MSW students. From all these people I have learned much. Throughout this project, I have been most grateful to my wife, Regina Yutzy-Wolfer, for her steady encouragement, support, forbearance, and love.

Together, we have many people to thank, beginning with the case reporters who provided detailed information about actual difficult situations from their professional experience. Without their thorough and self-reflective reporting, this collection would obviously not be possible. We also thank the case authors, many of whom tackled a new style of writing and persisted through multiple revisions to ensure the accuracy and clarity of these accounts. In that regard, we also value the helpful feedback from seven anonymous reviewers. We appreciate Lisa Gebo and Caroline Concilla of Brooks/Cole for their enthusiasm for and support of this new approach to case writing, and to the teams at Buuji and at ITC for their steady help with preparing the manuscript.

We hope that you will find this casebook a useful resource for class discussions that help you practice "thinking like a social worker." Jump in, the water's fine.

About the Editors

T. Laine Scales, Ph.D., is an associate professor of Social Work at Baylor University in Waco, Texas. She has authored, co-authored, or co-edited seven books including *Spirituality and Religion in Social Work Practice: Decision Cases with Teaching Notes* (CSWE, 2002) and *Rural Social Work: Building and Sustaining Community Assets* (Wadsworth, 2004); and *Decision Cases for Advanced Social Work Practice: Thinking Like a Social Worker* (Thomson-Brooks/Cole 2006). She has published over twenty articles and chapters in social work, higher education, and women's studies. Dr. Scales currently serves as an associate editor for the journal *Social Work and Christianity.* She has held leadership positions in the National Association of Social Workers, Texas Chapter. Prior to joining the faculty of Baylor, Dr. Scales taught at Stephen F. Austin State University in Nacogdoches, Texas, and Palm Beach Atlantic College in West Palm Beach, Florida.

Terry A. Wolfer, Ph.D., is an associate professor in the College of Social Work at the University of South Carolina (Columbia). He has authored or coauthored 20 articles and several additional manuscripts on social work education, faith-based social services, and psychological trauma. He co-edited *Spirituality and Religion in Social Work Practice: Decision Cases with Teaching Notes* (CSWE, 2002) and *Decision Cases for Advanced Social Work Practice: Thinking Like a Social Worker* (Thomson-Brooks/Cole, 2006). He is incoming editor for the journal Areté and currently serves as an associate editor for the journal *Social Work and Christianity.* He is a recipient of the Social Work Leadership

Development Award from the Project on Death in America for writing a collection of decision cases on death and dying in social work practice. Dr. Wolfer has served on the boards of several social service and professional organizations. He recently completed a sabbatical as a visiting scholar at the University of Queensland (Brisbane, Australia). Before joining the faculty at South Carolina, Dr. Wolfer was a visiting instructor at the University of Illinois at Chicago and a lecturer at the University of Chicago.

Case Author Biographies

Pat Gleason-Wynn, Ph.D., is a Lecturer in the School of Social Work at Baylor University in Waco, Texas. Her primary area of interest is gerontology with a particular focus on nursing home social work where she has practiced for almost 25 years. She has developed and leads a number of continuing education and professional development courses for gerontological social workers. She provides consultation to numerous nursing homes in Texas.

Debbie Gove, MSW., is a Renal Social Worker at Dialysis Clinic, Inc. and adjunct faculty member at Stephen F. Austin State University in Nacogdoches, Texas. Formerly, she served as Client Services Director at a rural agency that provides services to clients diagnosed with HIV/AIDS.

Helen Wilson Harris, MSW., is Senior Lecturer and Director of Field Education at Baylor University's School of Social Work. Helen teaches in both the baccalaureate and graduate programs. She was the founding director of Community Hospice of Waco and has 8 years of practice experience in residential child care and foster care and adoptions. Helen writes and presents in the areas of grief and loss and intergenerational practice.

Barbara Heard-Mueller, Ph.D., is a Visiting Assistant Professor in the School of Social Work at Stephen F. Austin State University, Nacogdoches, Texas. She has taught in social work and sociology for 14 years and has over 20 years of practice experience in public and private agencies and in private practice. She has done consultation with Community Action Nacogdoches Head Start Child Development Center developing strategic plans and needs assessments in East Texas. She has published several articles and chapters on aging and health care issues.

Mackenzi A. Huyser, Ph.D., is Chair of the Social Work Department at Trinity Christian College, Palos Heights, Illinois. Prior to her position at Trinity she worked in the field of child welfare, both in mentoring programs and home based services. She currently teaches undergraduate research and policy. Her current research interests include faculty participation in and institutional commitment to the scholarship of engagement.

Linda Morales, Ph.D., is the Director of the School of Social Work at Stephen F. Austin State University, Nacogdoches, Texas. She has been teaching for more than 16 years in MSW and BSW programs, and is an advanced clinical practitioner with many years experience in the mental health arena. She writes and presents articles, chapters, and decision cases on rural social work.

Susan Murty, Ph.D., is Associate Professor and MSW Program Coordinator at the School of Social Work at the University of Iowa. Her research focuses on rural service delivery, rural community practice, network analysis, intergenerational service learning, and domestic violence. She has developed an end-of-life care curriculum in the MSW Program with support from a Social Work Leadership Development Award received from the Project on Death in America. Her most recent project is gathering oral histories from Latino elders in Mexico.

Mary Anne Poe, MSW., is Associate Professor and Chair of the Department of Social Work, Union University, Jackson, Tennessee. She has taught social work at Union for eight years in the BSW program. She has worked previously in faith-based settings with children and families and has done consultation for faith-based agencies. Her research interests and teaching areas include social justice and development of cultural competence.

F. Matthew Schobert, Jr., M.Div., MSW., is unit manager of a structured-care home unit for adolescent boys at Methodist Children's Home, Waco, Texas. He provides case management and clinical services to youth and families. He lectures in the Baylor Interdisciplinary Core Program at Baylor University in Waco, Texas and serves on the board of directors at World Hunger Relief, Inc. He is an Assistant Editor of the journal *Social Work and Christianity* and has published several decision cases, articles, and chapters, and over a dozen book reviews in social work and in theology.

Scott W. Taylor, MSW., M.Div., is Lecturer in the School of Social Work, Baylor University, Waco, TX, where he teaches research methods for both undergraduate and graduate students. He has co-authored articles in *International Encyclopedia of Marriage and Family* (2002 MacMillan) as well as a book chapter in *Christianity and Social Work* (2nd ed., 2002, NACSW). His research interests include international social welfare, peace and social justice, and the intersection of faith and culture.

Sharon B. Templeman, Ph.D., is an Assistant Professor in the Stephen F. Austin State University School of Social Work, Nacogdoches, Texas where she has taught in the graduate and undergraduate programs for 7 years. Prior to teaching, Dr. Templeman practiced social work in the areas of child welfare, and mental health for 20 years. Currently her primary areas of research and publication are in rural and international social work.

Duncan T. Whyte, Ph.D., has taught in the graduate and undergraduate social work programs at the University of South Carolina and Columbia College (SC). He was formerly a Social Work Officer in the Unites States Army where he worked extensively in the areas of child protection and domestic violence. In addition to case method teaching, his research interests include critical thinking, school social work, and interpersonal violence.

Laura E. Zumdahl, M.A., is Lead Staff at Bethany Christian Services, Fond du Lac, Wisconsin. She is a 2004 graduate of the University of Chicago, School of Social Service Administration. Previous work experience includes program development in social work education, domestic violence, and medical social work. Her research interests include nonprofit management, program development, and church social work.

PART I

About Decision Cases

Chapter 1

An Introduction
to Decision Cases and
Case Method Learning

TERRY A. WOLFER

"Good judgment comes from experience.
Experience comes from bad judgment"

WALTER WRISTON
(CITED IN BRUNER, 1999, p. xxiii)

The case method of learning typically involves in–depth class discussions based on detailed, open-ended accounts of actual practice situations. These accounts, referred to as decision cases, require students to formulate the problems and decide on potential courses of action. The case analyses and class discussions help students learn to apply theory to practice and to develop important problem-solving and critical-thinking skills. Because this particular form of cases may be unfamiliar to you, we intend this introductory chapter to provide background information on cases and the case method. This chapter will do the following:

1. Consider the prevalence of cases in generalist social work education and practice.

2. Differentiate cases for decision making from the more common cases for examples or illustration.

3. Help students understand how case discussions differ, both philosophically and practically, from traditional approaches to social work education.

4. Identify general learning outcomes associated with analyzing and discussing decision cases, and the importance of these outcomes for social work practice.

5. Explain where these cases came from, and how they were written.

In the next chapter, we provide concrete tips for analyzing and preparing to discuss cases.

WHAT IS YOUR EXPERIENCE WITH CASES?

No doubt, you are well acquainted with the use of cases in your social work program. Many social work instructors and textbook authors provide cases to aid your understanding of social work practice. In field supervision, you likely discuss individual cases and the problems or challenges these pose for you. In your field practicum or social work employment, you may measure your workload in terms of the number of cases you carry at any point in time.

This collection of cases is similar in some ways to these various types of cases but different in other important ways. Like cases in your classrooms or textbooks, these cases were developed for teaching purposes. However, these cases have a more specific teaching purpose that probably differs from published cases with which you may be familiar. In social work education, most published cases have an illustrative purpose. They provide examples of good practice, or even exemplars for you to emulate. Such cases depict difficult practice situations and show how social workers dealt with these situations. They typically show how a social work theory was applied in the particular situation, providing insight or understanding, or how a social work intervention was carried out, providing guidance in use of the intervention. In short, such cases show you how some theory or intervention applies to practice or, more simply, how the theory or intervention *works*.

Discussing cases with your social work field instructor or supervisor also has a teaching purpose, though it might be more accurate to refer to this as a learning purpose. In supervision, your field instructor "looks over your shoulder" to ensure that things are going well and to provide direction as necessary. When you discuss difficult cases with your field instructor, you may review what has happened, what you have tried to do, and so on. Initially, your supervisor carries important responsibility for guiding your efforts. But as you gain practice experience, you will increasingly use supervision to make collaborative decisions about what to do next. In these situations, your field instructor or supervisor is not directing your work so much as helping you decide how to proceed, what to try, what the likely consequences will be, and so on. This type of supervision shifts the focus from the past to the present and future, from what happened to what to do next. And it shifts the emphasis from your instructor "teaching you what to do" to the two of you (or the supervision group) collaboratively figuring out what to do. This approach to supervision is common in professional social work practice, and this set of decision cases is intended to resemble and promote it.

In direct practice settings especially, the set of cases (caseload) for which you have responsibility also provides a shorthand way of referring to your workload.

In this usage, a case refers to the client system for which you have some professional responsibility. The client may be understood to be an individual, a couple, or a family unit.

In this casebook, however, the word *case* does not refer to cases of this type. Instead, we use *case* for referring to specific situations in professional practice that pose problems and dilemmas, and these situations are more like those described in the paragraph on supervision above. Furthermore, these cases come from generalist social work practice. As a result, the client system may include a program, organization, or community, in addition to individuals, families, or groups. This brief reflection reveals how prevalent cases are in professional social work practice, and also alerts us to some important distinctions in use of the term *case*.

CASES IN SOCIAL WORK EDUCATION

The use of cases is nothing new. For more than 100 years, social work instructors have used cases in the classroom to educate students (Fisher, 1978; Reitmeier, 2002; e.g., Reynolds, 1942; Towle, 1954). Over time, these cases have taken many forms, ranging from brief vignettes of only a few sentences or paragraphs complex book-length accounts.

Merseth (1996) identified three basic educational purposes for using cases: as examples or exemplars to illustrate practice, as foci for reflecting on practice, or as opportunities to practice decision making. For the first purpose, mentioned above, cases provide concrete and specific examples of how professional theories or interventions apply in practice situations. As illustrations, cases can help students understand theoretical content and practice skills. During the past few decades, most of the available social work casebooks provide cases for this purpose (e.g., Amodeo, Schofield, Duffy, Jones, Zimmerman, & Delgado, 1997; Haulotte & Kretzschmar, 2001; LeCroy, 1999; McClelland, Austin, & Este, 1998; Rivas & Hull, 2000).

Although most cases in social work education have an illustrative purpose, the cases here have primarily a decision-making purpose. They resemble the type of cases that social workers take to their supervisors when they are uncertain how to understand a situation or how to respond. In fact, the cases in this collection troubled the practitioners who experienced and reported them. For some, the situations remain perplexing months (and even years) after they occurred.

Rather than provide good examples of how practice theories or interventions might work, these cases present challenging problem-solving opportunities. As a result, they provide opportunities for you to practice decision making, to refine the skills you need in social work practice. Like social work practice dilemmas you might take to a supervisor, these cases present messy, ambiguous, problematic situations that invite and merit professional thinking and intervention. Discussing these challenging cases will clarify the fundamental importance of problem framing or formulation; they require you to bring structure to complex, ill-structured situations. Having formulated the problems, you must decide what to do about the various situations. As you will see, many social work interventions may be possible or even relevant in particular cases, but these interventions will vary by the extent to which they actually help resolve the basic dilemmas. Class discussions will clarify the probable consequences of various formulations and strategies, and help you refine your decision-making processes.

DISTINGUISHING DECISION CASES
FROM OTHER TYPES

In defining decision cases, scholars note several characteristics that distinguish them from other types of cases. For example, Mauffette-Leenders, Erskine, and Leenders (1997) define a decision case as "a description of an actual situation, commonly involving a decision, a challenge, an opportunity, a problem or issue faced by a person (or persons) in an organization. The case allows [the reader] to step figuratively into the position of the particular decision maker" (p. 2). Similarly, Christensen and Hansen (1987) define a decision case as:

> a partial, historical, clinical study of a situation which has confronted a . . . [practitioner]. Presented in narrative form to encourage student involvement, it provides data—substantive and process—essential to an analysis of a specific situation, for the framing of alternative action programs, and for their implementation recognizing the complexity and ambiguity of the practical world. (p. 27)

These definitions highlight several key characteristics of decision cases.

Like case examples or exemplars, decision cases provide accounts of social work practice situations but they differ in several important ways (Wolfer, 2003). Perhaps most distinctively, decision cases involve a dilemma of some sort for the practitioner and the written cases end with the situation unresolved (Leenders, Maufette-Leenders, & Erskine, 2001; Lynn, 1999; Weaver, Kowalski, & Pfaller, 1994). As a result, students must "untangle situations that are complex and undefined and impose a coherence of their own making" (Barnes, 1989, p. 17; cited in Merseth, 1996, p. 729). By presenting incomplete and ill-structured or "messy" situations (Boehrer & Linsky, 1990), decision cases especially stimulate readers to analyze the information they contain and formulate problems, and then to decide how to intervene in the situations. In short, open-ended cases spur readers to seek resolution.

Furthermore, decision cases generally depict actual situations encountered by social work practitioners rather than generic or composite situations.

Although some identifying information may be disguised to protect individuals and organizations, case writers try to avoid making any changes to cases that alter case dynamics (Cossom, 1991). Indeed, case writers construct decision cases based on multiple interviews with key participants, usually the protagonist and sometimes other people (Leenders, et al., 2001; Lynn, 1999; Naumes & Naumes, 1999; Welsh, 1999). Case writers gather detailed information, including conversational dialogue as case reporters remember it (Weaver et al., 1994). As a result, cases reflect the perspectives of case reporters, with both the strengths and limitations of their subjectivity. Well-written cases "put the student reader squarely in the shoes of the social worker" (Cossom, 1991, p. 141). They allow readers to "inhabit" or empathize with the world of the case reporter, to both know and "feel" the information that constitutes the problematic situation.

Decision cases typically differ from example cases in several additional ways. They often include more background information than example cases, including details about the time period, the social service agency and other organizations involved, organizational and social policies, and the community setting. In this way, cases better reflect the "complex, messy, context-specific activity" of professional practice (Merseth, 1996, p. 728). As experienced practitioners recognize, such information often plays an essential role in situations and their possible resolution (Doyle, 1990; Shulman, 1992). However, some of the included case details may be extraneous and potentially distracting, requiring readers to sort through the data, just as they must do in actual practice (Weaver et al., 1994).

Typically, decision cases also include more information about the protagonists (social workers) than example cases, because this information also plays an essential part in the situations (Weaver et al., 1994; Wolfer, 2003). Where example cases often invite readers to identify with a nondescript social worker (i.e., "Ms. Green"), decision cases provide details about the social worker's personal and professional circumstances that may be relevant for case dynamics. Putting this information on the page helps readers to recognize and consider how the self of the social worker may interact with problems and their resolution. Further, it encourages readers to reflect on how their own selves may also have consequences in professional practice.

Usually, decision cases do not include much theoretical content, except when case reporters explicitly mention it themselves. In professional practice, most situations do not present with explicit theoretical frameworks (Lynn, 1999; Sykes & Bird, 1992). Decision cases simply reflect that lack of explicit theory. As a result, the raw case data requires that readers supply theory for understanding the situations and helps them come to understand the critical need to do so (i.e., theory provides a "handle" on case situations). It also allows instructors considerable latitude in discussing cases from different theoretical perspectives.

These cases may provide little new information about topics you have been learning in other courses (though you may learn about particular social work settings, interventions, or problems with which you are unfamiliar). Instead, they emphasize the use of previous learning, especially in novel situations. In that way, these cases resemble social work practice, and discussing these cases resembles peer supervision. The cases themselves seldom make clear what theory or interventions might be suitable. You must decide about that, drawing from what you have learned up to this point. Hopefully, by providing opportunities for you to practice decision making in complex and challenging situations, analyzing and discussing the cases will also help you to refine your decision-making skills and to become a more self-reflective decision maker. Some of the things you will learn from discussing these cases would likely have occurred during your initial years of social work employment. But by discussing these cases, you can accelerate your learning and aid your successful transition to professional social work practice.

For these reasons, this collection of decision cases is especially well suited for use in capstone courses or integrative field seminars. For all students, these cases help provide a bridge between theory and practice, between the classroom and their agency settings. For students nearing completion of their educational programs, these cases may assist their transition from student to practitioner as they assume greater decision-making responsibility.

OUTCOMES OF DECISION CASE LEARNING

In part, the differences between novices and experienced practitioners may have less to do with what they know than with how they use their knowledge (Livingston & Borko, 1989). Business educators Barnes, Christensen, and Hansen (1994) argue that case method instruction helps to develop in students an applied "administrative point of view" (p. 50). In other words, case method instruction helps business students to develop the perspective of experienced business administrators or practitioners. In social work, we could refer to this as "thinking like a social worker" (hence the title of this book).

Barnes, Christensen, and Hansen (1994) suggest that an administrative point of view includes several components. These components are (1) a focus on understanding the specific context; (2) a sense for appropriate boundaries; (3) sensitivity to interrelationships; (4) examining and understanding any situation from a multidimensional point of view; (5) accepting personal responsibility for the solution of organizational problem; and (6) an action orientation (pp. 50–51). These components reflect a thoroughly systemic approach to understanding practice.

Furthermore, the latter component, (6) above, an action orientation, includes several dimensions acquired through practice experience. These dimensions are (a) a sense of the possible; (b) willingness to make decisions on the basis of imperfect and limited data; (c) a sense of the critical aspects of a situation; (d) the ability to combine discipline and creativity; (e) skill in converting targets into accomplishments; and (f) an appreciation of the major limitations of professional action (p. 51). Together, they distinguish expert practitioners from novices. In short, the concept of an administrative or practitioner point of view redirects our attention from what students know to their ability to use their knowledge judiciously. From this perspective, theoretical knowledge and technical skill are essential but insufficient for competent practice. Not only must competent professionals have knowledge and skills, they must know how to use these, and exercise good judgment in doing so.

Although the knowledge, skill, and value bases differ significantly between business and social work, we think there are some important parallels between how business and social work professionals need to think and act in professional practice. As Barnes and his colleagues argue (1994), competent practice requires profoundly systemic ways of thinking and deciding. Hopefully, analyzing and discussing these cases will help you to acquire some of the attitudes, knowledge, and skills that experienced social workers identify as critical to their professional success.

Several teacher educators identify other outcomes of case method learning. At the most basic level, cases convey information or declarative knowledge, that is, *what* to know. For example, education researchers have explored the effectiveness of cases for introducing multicultural perspectives, pedagogical theory, and mathematics content (e.g., Merseth, 1996). At a deeper level, cases can promote different ways of thinking or procedural knowledge, that is, *how* to know and do. For example, education researchers have begun to explore the effectiveness of cases for developing problem-solving and decision-making skills, beliefs about professional authority and personal efficacy, more realistic perspectives on the complexities of practice (and new ways of looking at practice), and habits of reflection (Merseth, 1996).

Lundeberg (1999), another teacher educator, provides an alternative conceptual framework for understanding case method learning outcomes. Based on empirical research, she reports benefits in five categories, most of which relate to different ways of thinking. The first category, theoretical and practical understandings, combines two kinds of knowledge that researchers have often separated. She combines them because of the ways instructors can use cases for generating theory from practice, encouraging students to apply theory in practical situations, and for helping students discover when and how theories may be useful (p. 4). The second category, improved reasoning and reflective decision making, reflects a basic purpose of case method instruction. Decision cases are specifically designed for helping students develop their abilities: "to identify, frame, or find a problem; consider problems from multiple perspectives; provide solutions for problems identified; and consider the consequences and ethical ramifications of these solutions" (p. 8). As another teacher educator notes, "Many students see problems as no more than common-sense, obvious difficulties. They have not developed the idea that problems are constructed and can be constructed in more and less fruitful ways" (Kleinfield, 1991, p. 7; cited in Lundeberg, 1999, p. 9). Case discussions provide significant opportunities for developing more sophisticated decision-making abilities. The growth of reasoning relates to a third category, metacognition, the process of reflecting on one's own thinking processes (Lundeberg, 1999, p. 12). While awareness of thinking and learning processes is obviously important for classroom teachers, it has an important parallel for social workers. Thinking and learning processes are part of a broader category of change processes. Case discussions may help students better understand the nature and difficulty of change processes, especially as they become more self-reflective regarding their own learning. For education students, metacognitions are closely related to a fourth category, beliefs about learning (p. 14). Early literature on cognitive change suggested that awareness of one's own beliefs and how they conflicted with empirically based ideas about learning would lead to change in beliefs. More recent literature reveals that cognitive change is less rational and more dependent on social interaction. Applying this insight to change processes more generally, the case method may provide experience and insight regarding the importance of relationship dynamics in social work interventions, whether at the micro or macro level. Lundeberg refers to a final category of benefits as social, ethical, and epistemological growth (p. 15). Her colleague, Harrington (1994), wrote:

> The knowledge of most worth is brought into being dialogically. It is said and heard in multiple ways—transformed in the sharing—enriched through multiplicity. Dialogue allows students to become aware of what they share in common, as well as the uniqueness of each of them as individuals. (p. 192; cited in Lundeberg, 1999, p. 16)

Deep appreciation for dialogue, as a means of comprehending similarity and difference, represents a profound type of growth fostered by case method. Dialogue is relevant for social work practice with clients but also for interaction with colleagues, agencies, and communities. And it leads to greater appreciation for the ethical context of practice. In their book, Lundeberg and her colleagues review the empirical evidence for these benefits of case method learning (Lundeberg, Levin, & Harrington, 1999).

Although originally identified in the context of teacher education, these benefits of case method learning seem highly relevant for social work practice as well. Competent practice requires both theoretical and practical knowledge, reasoning and reflective decision-making skills, metacognitive awareness (especially regarding change processes), appropriate beliefs about change, and social, ethical, and epistemological growth. Unfortunately, these significant benefits of case method learning are sometimes overlooked in social work education, or at least not addressed in formal ways. In that respect, the case method may prove to be a valuable supplement to the traditional classroom.

CASE METHOD TEACHING

To most fully exploit the teaching potential of decision cases, instructors must use a "case method teaching" approach (Barnes, Christensen, & Hansen, 1994; Cossom, 1991; Erskine, Leenders, & Mauffette-Leenders, 1998; Lundeberg, Levin, & Harrington, 1999; Lynn, 1999; Welty, 1989). Because this approach may differ from what your instructors normally do, it may be helpful for you to have some advance warning about what they may do differently and to be aware of their reasons for it. Case method teaching relies heavily on discussion, and case method instructors essentially lead discussions by asking questions (Boehrer & Linsky, 1990). The overarching questions are twofold: What is the problem? And what would you do about it? In classroom discussions, however, instructors may not actually ask these two basic questions. Instead, they ask many more specific questions designed to explore these two questions. Instructors formulate and select questions based partly on their instructional goals, what background knowledge students bring to the discussion, and the direction and flow of the immediate discussion. As discussions develop, instructors may encourage individual students to elaborate on their perspectives, seek divergent viewpoints from other students, and ask about connections or discrepancies between new comments and previous comments. Although it sometimes frustrates students, case method instructors consistently refrain from providing their own perspectives or opinions about the cases. Rather than identify possible errors of fact or judgment themselves, instructors promote critical thinking by asking good questions. Indeed, case method instructors consider students' increasing ability to pose good questions to be important evidence of their learning (Boehrer & Linsky, 1990).

Much like small group leaders, case method instructors also must attend to the level of discussion process (Lundeberg, Levin, & Harrington, 1999; Welty, 1989). For example, instructors seek to distribute speaking turns, steering the discussion away from overly talkative students toward quieter students. They monitor perceptions of classroom safety, and consider the effects of their own and students' contributions. In their questioning, they sometimes push students to express disagreements and at other times allow students to go more slowly. More than some other teaching approaches, case method teaching requires that instructors listen well (Christensen, 1991; Leonard, 1991), to maintain simultaneous awareness of both discussion content and discussion process.

THE CASES

This book includes a diverse mix of cases, some involving predominantly micro settings and issues and others involving predominantly mezzo or macro settings and issues. In ways that may surprise you, however, you will come to see how micro, mezzo, and macro issues are frequently intertwined in generalist practice. These cases make clear the systemic nature of reality and provide support for the widespread emphasis on systems thinking in social work education. We created the mix of cases to reinforce this point.

Occasionally, some students object to the mix of cases. Students who may be more interested in micro practice, for example, may not understand why they should know or care about the characteristics of a rural community. Or students who may be more interested in macro practice may not understand why they should be familiar with practice interventions for individual clients. Hopefully, this collection will help you to see common threads across these situations, to develop your skills of assessment and decision making, and to better understand the interactive nature of systems. Hopefully, discussing these cases also will help you to practice generalist social work with increased insight, flexibility, and creativity. These assertions may prompt you to wonder about the intended benefits of learning with decision cases.

WHERE THESE CASES CAME FROM, AND HOW THEY WERE WRITTEN

Because we intended the cases for students in the final semester of an undergraduate social work program, the cases all involve BSW-level practitioners. To qualify for use in the course and inclusion in this case collection, cases must have met several criteria:[1]

1. The situation may be drawn from any field of social work practice.

2. The situation may be drawn from generalist practice with individuals, families, groups, organizations or communities.

3. The situation must include a social worker with some critical decision-making responsibility (the social worker serves as the protagonist).

4. The situation must involve some type of dilemma for the social worker. The dilemma may include, for example, conflicting values or ethical principles held by individual clients, their families, the social worker, the social work organization, or social policies. In the best cases, competent social workers may disagree about appropriate responses to the dilemma.

---

1. The final case, The Ideal Client, is one exception to these criteria in that the social worker was an MSW-level worker in advanced practice. We included this case because the worker's concerns and dilemmas in the beginning phase of treatment seem applicable to generalist practice.

5. The social worker must have (or be working toward) an undergraduate social work degree, so that BSW-level students can reasonably identify with and learn from his or her dilemma.

6. Finally, the social worker must be interested and willing to report the situation in confidential interviews with a case writer.

As implied by these criteria, the cases were all field researched. That is, they were all based on in-depth interviews with individual social workers who agreed to report their experiences. More specifically, the cases were researched and written in an interactive process consisting of several steps.

First, before the case reporting sessions, case reporters prepared brief written accounts of a problem or decision they actually faced in social work practice, or in some instances, recounted to case authors a decision or dilemma. These initial accounts helped case writers determine the likely appropriateness of case dilemmas before they began in-depth research.

Second, during the reporting sessions, case reporters told case writers the stories behind their accounts. Case writers audiotape-recorded these interviews to collect detailed descriptions and numerous direct quotes from case reporters.

Third, after the reporting sessions, the case writers prepared working drafts of the cases that included a title, an opening paragraph or introductory "hook," necessary background sections, and the story line with descriptions and quotes.

Fourth, case writers sought additional information from case reporters as needed, exchanged working drafts with the case reporters and editors for editorial feedback, and returned final drafts to the case reporters for confirmation. Case writers did not release cases for publication until case reporters signed release forms indicating they felt satisfied that the written cases accurately reflected their experiences and adequately disguised the situations.

In consultation with the case reporters, we disguised the cases to protect them, their clients, and their social service organizations. In most cases, the disguise involved changing names of people, organizations, and places, and selected details. As much as possible, however, we avoided changing case data that would alter essential case dynamics. For example, we did not change the gender or ethnicity of case reporters or clients, or the geographic regions in which cases occurred. In subtle ways, these and similar factors influence how the case situations developed and how they may be interpreted, and we did not want to undermine the reality of what the case reporters experienced. As suggested above, learning to take account of such details distinguishes expert practitioners from novices.

Whatever you think of particular decision cases in the collection, avoid jumping to conclusions. The case reporters have been generous and courageous in telling about particularly challenging, even troubling situations they have faced in professional practice. For that, we are most grateful. For some case reporters, the situations continue to frustrate, perplex, and concern them, and that was part of the reason they agreed to report their cases.

READING THE CASES

The decision cases in this collection can be read on several levels. On one level, they simply depict a variety of settings that employ social workers and the types of situations that occasionally crop up in those settings. Obviously, the cases represent only a small sample of practice fields and settings (e.g., medical social work, probation, school social work, international social work).

On a second level, the cases depict specific challenges that individual social workers encountered in certain settings and at certain points in time. From a systems perspective, the multiple and overlapping factors will be quite evident, though the specifics vary from case to case. In various combinations, these factors include client needs and values; social worker needs, values and skills; needs and values of other individuals related to the clients; organizational philosophies, policies, and procedures; professional social work values and ethics; and government policies and laws. These multiple factors create the complex and particular environments in which social workers must function, and which they must carefully consider when attempting to resolve the dilemmas.

But on a third, more abstract level, the cases also reflect common challenges of social work practice across settings (and, we might add, of human experience). These challenges include, for example, balancing client and organizational needs, resolving contradictory policy requirements, making decisions with incomplete information, identifying the appropriate limits of professional intervention, anticipating unintended consequences of decisions, and resolving value or ethical dilemmas.

As you read, try to consider the cases on each of these levels. You may begin by asking yourself, "What is this case about?" Repeatedly asking and answering this question can help you reach for deeper levels of understanding. The next chapter goes further in suggesting ways to read and analyze the cases and to prepare for discussing them.

REFERENCES

Amodeo, M., Schofield, R., Duffy, T., Jones, K., Zimmerman, T., & Delgado, M. (Eds.). (1997). *Social work approaches to alcohol and other drug problems: Case studies and teaching tools.* Alexandria, VA: Council on Social Work Education.

Barnes, L. B., Christensen, C. R., & Hansen, A. J. (1994). *Teaching and the case method* (3rd ed.). Boston: Harvard Business School Press.

Boehrer, J., & Linsky, M. (1990). Teaching with cases: Learning to question. In M. D. Svinicki (Ed.), *The changing face of college teaching* (pp. 41–57). San Francisco: Jossey-Bass.

Bruner, R. F. (1999). Note to the student: How to study and discuss cases. In *Case studies in finance: Managing for corporate value creation* (3rd ed.; pp. xxiii–xxvi). Boston: Irwin McGraw-Hill. [Also available online at http://faculty.darden.virginia.edu/brunerb/resources_studentnote.htm]

Christensen, C. R. (1991). The discussion teacher in action: Questioning, listening, and response. In C. R. Christensen,

D. A. Garvin, & A. Sweet (Eds.), *Education for judgment: The artistry of discussion leadership* (pp. 153–172). Boston: Harvard Business School Press.

Christensen, C. R., & Hansen, A. (1987). *Teaching and the case method*. Boston: Harvard Business School Press.

Cossom, J. (1991). Teaching from cases: Education for critical thinking. *Journal of Teaching in Social Work, 5*(1), 139–155.

Doyle, W. (1990). Case methods in the education of teachers. *Teacher Education Quarterly, 17*(1), 7–16.

Erskine, J. A., Leenders, M. R., & Mauffette-Leenders, L. A. (1998). *Teaching with cases* (3rd ed.). London, ONT: Ivey Publishing, Ivey School of Business Administration, The University of Western Ontario.

Fisher, C. F. (1978). Being there vicariously by case studies. In M. Ohmer and Associates (Ed.), *On college teaching: A guide to contemporary practices* (pp. 258–285). San Francisco: Jossey-Bass.

Harrington, H. (1994). Teaching and knowing. *Journal of Teacher Education, 45*(3), 190–198.

Haulotte, S. M., & Kretzschmar, J. A. (Eds.). (2001). *Case scenarios for teaching and learning social work practice*. Alexandria, VA: Council on Social Work Education.

LeCroy, C. W. (1999). *Case studies in social work practice* (2nd ed.). Pacific Grove, CA: Brooks/Cole.

Leenders, M. R., Mauffette-Leenders, L. A., & Erskine, J. A. (2001). *Writing cases* (4th ed.). London, ONT: Ivey Publishing, Ivey School of Business Administration, The University of Western Ontario.

Leonard, H. B. (1991). With open ears: Listening and the art of discussion leading. In C. R. Christensen, D. A. Garvin, & A. Sweet (Eds.), *Education for judgment: The artistry of discussion leadership* (pp. 137–151). Boston: Harvard Business School Press.

Livingston, C., & Borko, H. (1989). Expert-novice difference in teaching: A cognitive analysis and implications for teacher education. *Journal of Teacher Education, 40*(4), 36–42.

Lundeberg, M. A. (1999). Discovering teaching and learning through cases. In M. A. Lundeberg, B. B. Levin, & H. L. Harrington (Eds.), *Who learns what from cases and how? The research base for teaching with cases* (pp. 3–23). Mahwah, NJ: Lawrence Erlbaum.

Lundeberg, M. A., Levin, B. B., & Harrington, H. L. (1999). *Who learns what from cases and how? The research base for teaching with cases*. Mahwah, NJ: Lawrence Erlbaum.

Lynn, L. E., Jr. (1999). *Teaching and learning with cases: A guidebook*. New York: Chatham House.

Mauffette-Leenders, L. A., Erskine, J. A., & Leenders, M. R. (1997). *Learning with cases*. London, ONT: Ivey Publishing, Ivey School of Business Administration, The University of Western Ontario.

McClelland, R. W., Austin, C. D., & Este, D. (1998). *Macro case studies in social work*. Milwaukee: Families International.

Merseth, K. K. (1996). Cases and case methods in teacher education. In J. Sikula & T. J. Buttery & E. Guyton (Eds.), *Handbook of research on teacher education* (2nd ed., pp. 722–744). New York: Simon & Schuster Macmillan.

Naumes, W., & Naumes, M. J. (1999). *The art and craft of case writing*. Thousand Oaks, CA: Sage.

Reitmeier, M. (2002). *Use of cases in social work education*. Unpublished manuscript, University of South Carolina, Columbia.

Reynolds, B. C. (1942). *Learning and teaching in the practice of social work*. New York: Farrar & Rinehart.

Rivas, R. F., & Hull, G. H. (2000). *Case studies in generalist practice* (2nd ed.). Pacific Grove, CA: Brooks/Cole.

Shulman, L. S. (1992). Toward a pedagogy of cases. In J. Shulman (Ed.), *Case methods in teacher education* (pp. 1–30). New York: Teachers College Press.

Sykes, G., & Bird, T. (1992). Teacher education and the case idea. In G. Grant (Ed.), *Review of Research in Education* (Vol. 18, pp. 457–521). Washington, DC: American Educational Research Association.

Towle, C. (1954). *The learner in education for the professions: As seen in education for social work*. Chicago: University of Chicago Press.

Weaver, R. A., Kowalski, T. J., & Pfaller, J. E. (1994). Case-method teaching. In K. W. Prichard & R. M. Sawyer (Eds.), *Handbook of college teaching: Theory and applications* (pp. 171–178). Westport, CT: Greenwood.

Welsh, M. F. (1999). A technique for cross-cultural case research and writing. In H. E. Klein (Ed.), *Interactive teaching and the multimedia revolution: Case method & other techniques* (pp. 3–9). Madison, WI: Omni.

Welty, W. M. (1989). Discussion method teaching: A practical guide. *To Improve the Academy, 8,* 197–216. [For a briefer version, see: Welty, W. M. (1989). Discussion method teaching: How to make it work. *Change, 21*(4), 40–49.]

Wolfer, T. A. (2003). Decision cases for Christians in social work: Introduction to the special issue. *Social Work & Christianity, 30*(2), 103–116.

Wolfer, T. A., Freeman, M. L., & Rhodes, R. (2001). Developing and teaching an MSW capstone course using case methods of instruction. *Advances in Social Work, 2*(2), 156–171.

Chapter 2

Tips for Learning
from Decision Cases

TERRY A. WOLFER
T. LAINE SCALES

W hat you get out of reading, analyzing, and discussing a particular case depends largely on the method and thoroughness of your preparation. The following chapter provides sequential tips regarding effective processes for reading and analyzing cases and for participating in decision case discussions. Some sections are drawn directly from a "Note to the Student" (Bruner, 1999), written by a master teacher for business students, while other sections were written for social work students specifically.

READING THE CASE

There are many ways to read cases. You can increase your reading effectiveness and efficiency by deliberately using different ways at various points in the process. From the very first reading, you can maximize your learning with a decision case by active, purposeful, and discriminating engagement. Bruner (1999) suggests:

> The very first time you read any case, look for the forest not the trees. This requires that your first reading be quick. Do not begin taking notes on the first round; instead, read the case like a magazine article. The first few paragraphs of a well-constructed case usually say something about the problem—read those carefully. Then quickly read the rest of the case,

seeking mainly a sense of the scope of the problems, and what information the case contains to help resolve them. Leaf through the exhibits, looking for what information they hold, rather than for any analytical insights. At the conclusion of the first pass, read any supporting articles or notes that your instructor may have recommended. (Bruner, 1999, pp. xxiii–xxiv)

This brief, initial review of the case will quickly orient you to the situation and its overall context.

DIGGING INTO THE CASE SITUATION: DEVELOP YOUR "AWARENESS"

Reading the case a second time will deepen your understanding, as Bruner (1999) reminds case readers:

With the broader perspective in mind, the second and more detailed reading will be more productive. The reason is that as you now encounter details, your mind will be able to organize them in some useful fashion rather than inventorying them randomly. Making linkages among case details is necessary toward solving the case. At this point you can take the notes that will set up your analysis. (Bruner, 1999, p. xxiv)

While your instructor may provide questions to aid your preparation for particular cases, you can promote your own analytic skills by learning to pose and answer questions of your own. To begin this process, try to keep the following generic questions in mind:

1. Who is the protagonist in the case? Who must take action on the problem? What does he or she have at stake? What pressures is he or she under?

2. What is the field of practice? Who are the usual clientele? What is the demand for services? How are services funded? What are the professional affiliations and qualifications of staff? What services do the social workers provide?

3. What are the organizational auspices (e.g., public, private nonprofit, private for-profit), and who has primary authority in the organization? With whom does it collaborate or compete? Is the organization comparatively strong or weak? In what ways?

4. What are the organization's goals or desired outcomes? If not a social work organization, how does social work contribute to its goals? What are the primary intervention methods used by the organization or, if not a social work organization, the social workers who work for it?

5. How well has the organization performed in pursuit of its goals? How clearly does the organization identify its goals?

At the outset, this may sound rather daunting. There is *so much* to consider! Understand that thinking of these factors will become more natural and routine as you become more acquainted with the process of analyzing cases. The goal here is to develop greater awareness of fundamental and perennial issues, and a routine habit of attending to them. As Bruner suggests, awareness is an important attribute of successful practitioners.

DEVELOP EMPATHIC UNDERSTANDING

When reading the case, seek empathic understanding of the situation from the protagonist's perspective. It may be helpful to imagine yourself as a personal consultant to the social worker in the case. As such, you need to "start where the social worker is," to paraphrase an old cliché. Take account of the social worker's background, experience, skills, thoughts, biases, and emotions, and also of your own. Because the particular case dilemmas often involve these very factors, it is not possible or appropriate to simply replace the protagonist with your self in the case situation. These factors cannot be wished away. Any solution must take account of them, much as a consultant or supervisor would do in actual practice.

Having read and reread the case—to get a sense of the story, develop your awareness, and empathize with the protagonist—you are ready to begin more deliberate analysis. Analysis may begin with an initial statement of the problem but beware of simply adopting the perspective of the protagonist or other participants in the case.

DEFINING OR FORMULATING
THE PROBLEM

Defining or formulating the problem represents one of the most important and challenging aspects of case analysis and discussion.

> A common trap for many [practitioners] is to assume that the issue at hand is the real problem most worthy of their time, rather than a symptom of some larger problem that really deserves their time. (Bruner, 1999, p. xxv)

Students tend to take the "presenting problem" at face value, whether it's posed in the case by the client or the social worker protagonist, and assume that it represents the real problem.

> Students who are new to the case method tend to focus narrowly in defining problems and often overlook the influence which the larger setting has on the problem. In doing this, the student develops narrow specialist habits, never achieving [a broader systems perspective]. It is useful and important for you to define the problem yourself, and in the process, validate the problem as suggested by the protagonist in the case. (p. xxv)

At this point in your analysis, it is also wise to define the problem tentatively. Treat your problem definition as a hypothesis to guide further analysis, a way to provide some structure for your thinking and questioning.

ANALYSIS: IDENTIFYING THE KEY ISSUES AND HOW THEY RELATE

The next, and most time-consuming stage involves careful analysis of the case. There are several things to understand here. First, "case analysis is often iterative: an understanding of the big issues invites an analysis of details—then the details may restructure the big issues and invite the analysis of other details. In some cases, getting to the 'heart of the matter' will mean just such iteration" (Bruner, 1999, p. xxv).

Second, when doing analysis, mental experiments often help to develop insight. For example, if the client is a man, you might consider how the case might be different if the client were a woman. Or, if the client is a person of color, consider how the situation might differ if she or he were white.

You can sometimes determine a factor's relevance by mentally subtracting it from the case and considering whether the problem goes away. If there is still a problem, then the particular factor has limited relevance. Compare contrasting definitions of the situation offered by people in the case, and ask yourself how else it may be construed.

Consider the client system and whether it could be defined differently. Brainstorm possible factors, on other system levels, that may cause or influence the situation. Identify what organizational policy may be relevant, unclear, or absent. Determine whether multiple ethical standards may be relevant. In short, play with definitions, comparisons, and contrasts.

Third, as you analyze the case, be prepared to revise your initial problem definition. Ask whether your emerging insights fit the problem definition. If not, try to redefine the problem in a way that accounts for your new insights. Redefining the problem requires that you reconsider other aspects of your analysis as well.

Fourth, understand that problem definition both guides analysis and also captures or reflects analysis. For most people, writing concise problem statements represents a major challenge. Skill in problem definition comes with practice and experience. "The best case students develop an instinct for where to devote their analysis. Economy of effort is desirable. If you have invested wisely in problem definition, economical analysis tends to follow" (Bruner, 1999, p. xxv). Carefully consider what belongs in the problem statement, versus what is important but not central to the problem, and therefore only belongs in the contextual analysis that supports it. Although these analytic processes can be tedious and time consuming, with practice you will become faster and more efficient.

PREPARE TO PARTICIPATE: TAKE A STAND

Eventually, you must shape your analysis of the situation into an argument for action.

> To develop analytical insights without making recommendations is useless to [practitioners], and drains the case study experience of some of its learning power. A stand means having a point of view about the problem, a recommendation, and an analysis to back up both of them. To prepare to take a stand, remember the words of Walt Disney: "Get a good idea and stay with it. Dog it and work at it until it's done, and done right." (Bruner, 1999, pp. xxv–xxvi)

Developing an argument for action requires courage; it represents a test of your case analysis. Often, there are many things at stake—especially for the client and social worker directly but also for the client's family members and associates and the social worker's organization, program, and co-workers. Despite these risks, you must choose how to act. In the world of practice, analysis that does not lead to action has limited value and may even be counterproductive.

Recognize, however, that if all students take stands, as they should, this will likely produce vigorous disagreements. Many students feel uncomfortable taking a stand, especially in the face of such disagreements. Having a strong desire to get along with their peers and instructors, they may downplay differences in their analysis or recommendations in order to reduce interpersonal tension. But this undermines the potential benefit of the process, for the group and also for the individual student. Without vigorous debate, the group may not consider diverse perspectives and students miss opportunities to practice introducing and defending their ideas. Developing the confidence and skill to assert yourself in group contexts will increase your effectiveness in family and group treatment settings, supervision sessions, meetings of professional teams, committees, or boards, or advocacy situations. In many situations, social workers will often agree and disagree. The case discussion process helps you practice doing so in direct and respectful ways.

THINGS TO AVOID WHILE PREPARING

When preparing for case discussions, there are several things to avoid. *Skipping or shortchanging preparation* will limit your ability to participate effectively in the discussion and, more importantly, will limit what you personally can learn from the discussion. You may find that reading decision cases for comprehension requires more careful and focused reading than you typically do with textbooks. *Endorsing the presenting problem* may seriously bias your analysis of the case, while *ignoring the presenting problem* reflects a failure to understand an important perspective in the case. *Focusing on either details or the big picture,* to the exclusion of the other, undermines your analysis. *Jumping to conclusions* without adequate evidence prematurely ends your analysis and risks gross mis-understanding of the case. On the other hand, *not drawing conclusions* about the problem and its resolution circumvents the challenge and purpose of decision cases, reducing the opportunity to exercise and develop your decision-making skills.

ACTIVELY SUPPORT YOUR CONCLUSIONS IN THE DISCUSSION, BUT STAY OPEN TO EMERGING INSIGHTS

As a result of preparing, you may come to the discussion having already for-mulated conclusions, sometimes very firm conclusions, about the nature of the problem and appropriate responses. Sharing your conclusions can benefit both you and your classmates, but you also must remain open to their conclusions and further insights that will emerge in the discussion.

> Of course, one can have a stand without the world being any wiser. To take a stand in case discussions means to participate actively in the discussion and to advocate your stand until new facts or analysis emerge to warrant a change. Learning by the case method is not a spectator sport. A classic error many students make is to bring into the case method classroom the habits of the lecture hall (i.e., passively absorbing what other people say). These habits fail miserably in the case method classroom because they only guarantee that one absorbs the truths and fallacies uttered by others. The purpose of [decision case method] is to develop and exercise one's own skills and judgment. This takes practice and participation, just as in a sport. Here are two good general suggestions: (1) defer significant note-taking until after class and (2) strive to contribute to every case discussion. (Bruner, 1999, p. xxvi)

In short, active participation is critical for your learning. But thoughtful responding to new insights, whether these come from you or other partici-pants, will be important, too.

LISTEN CAREFULLY

Effective participation in case discussion also requires that you listen carefully and actively. Concentrate on what others say, and on what they mean. Focus on their explicit content but also try to discern their underlying assumptions and values. The active listening skills you may have learned for social work prac-tice can apply in case discussion, too. You must gain adequate understanding, through careful listening, before you can make a fair evaluation. But do evaluate what you hear, comparing it with your own ideas. Do you agree? Why or why not? (Mauffette-Leenders, Erskine, & Leenders, 1998, p. 94). At the same time, guard against focusing on what you will say next because that undermines your ability to listen effectively.

MAKING CONTRIBUTIONS

During the case discussion, students may make either content contributions or process contributions (Mauffette-Leenders et al., 1998). Content contributions include separating facts from opinions, providing analysis, identifying reasonable assumptions, or offering an action plan. An example of a content contribution would be "The immediate issue is . . . and the basic issue is . . ." (p. 86). Process contributions, in contrast, refer to the structure of the discussion. They require careful listening and observation of how the discussion unfolds. Process contributions include clarifying questions, suggesting that a certain area of the case needs to be explored further, linking points raised earlier, or summarizing the discussion thus far. An example of a process contribution would be "We need to spend more (or less) time on . . ." or "We should hear from Hannah because . . ." (p. 86). You may recognize that process contributions are similar to comments an instructor or group facilitator makes. Ideally, you will learn to make both content and process contributions and also learn to recognize when either would be most appropriate and helpful. As you practice thinking like a social worker, you are practicing roles as an active member of a task group, or even as the facilitator. The point here is to contribute in various ways that move the discussion forward.

THINGS TO AVOID IN CASE DISCUSSIONS

When participating in case discussions, there are several things to avoid (Mauffette-Leenders et al., 1998, pp. 89–90). For example, *simply repeating case facts* contributes little to the discussion unless there is some confusion about the facts. *Repeating someone else's comments* reflects a failure to pay attention. *Inconsequential interjections* such as saying, "I agree," without explaining why contribute very little to the discussion. Likewise, *asking questions that divert the discussion* such as asking the instructor for his or her opinion may only delay or derail the discussion. Other *digressions* include irrelevant or out of place comments such as personal anecdotes that have little relevance to the situation. *Monopolizing the discussion* reflects an unwillingness to listen and learn from others. Sometimes students believe they have special understanding of case situations because of previous experience, and they actually do. Nevertheless, their understanding may be limited and biased by those insider perspectives.

In such cases, they may benefit from the comments and questions of others having less experience. In sharp contrast, *disengaged* students rarely contribute to the discussion or, when they do jump in, tend to make superficial or irrelevant comments. Finally, *uncivil behavior* such as attacking, ridiculing, or putting down other participants or their views can have a damaging effect on case discussions.

Though in different ways, students exhibiting dominant, disengaged, and uncivil behavior all limit the diversity of viewpoints available in a discussion. Dominating behavior limits the opportunities others have to participate, while uncivil behavior may frighten and discourage others from participating. Disengaged students simply withhold their own contributions.

TRUST THE PROCESS

Case discussions may be complex, unpredictable, and bewildering. As a result, you may wonder at times where a particular discussion is headed or what you are gaining from the process. Bruner (1999) offers some good advice:

> The learnings from a case-method course are impressive. They arrive cumulatively over time. In many cases, the learnings continue well after the course has finished. Occasionally, these learnings hit you with the force of a tsunami. But generally, the learnings creep in quietly, but powerfully, like the tide. After the case course, you will look back and see that your thinking, mastery, and appreciation for [social work] have changed dramatically. The key point is that you should not measure the success of your progress on the basis of any single case discussion. Trust that in the cumulative work over many cases you will gain the mastery you seek. (Bruner, 1999, p. xxvi)

With that in mind, you can hopefully maintain the kind of openness and engagement that contributes most to your learning and growth.

FOCUS ON HERE-AND-NOW PROCESS, AND RESULTS WILL FOLLOW

Bruner (1999) reminds us that the case method is an excellent way to develop and practice new ways of learning and thinking:

> View the case method experience as a series of opportunities to test your mastery of techniques and your [professional] judgment. If you seek a list of axioms to be etched in stone, you are bound to disappoint yourself. As in real life, there are virtually no "right" answers to these cases in the sense that a scientific or engineering problem has an exact solution.

Jeff Milman has said, "The answers worth getting are never found in the back of the book." What matters is that you obtain a way of thinking about [social work] situations that you can carry from one job (or career) to the next. In the case method it is largely true that how you learn is what you learn. (Bruner, 1999, p. xxvi)

MAINTAIN PERSPECTIVE

Because case method learning may be quite different from what you've experienced before, it's helpful to know that you may respond with strong emotions. These emotions may stem from unfamiliarity with the method and uncertainty about what to expect and how to participate, the unsettling nature of some case dilemmas, profound differences and conflicts that emerge in the case discussions, and the ambiguity of solutions and their likely consequences.

FINALLY, FOCUS ON
LONG-TERM OUTCOMES

At the same time, remember the learning outcomes identified in the previous chapter. These outcomes of case method learning can be quite significant overall, but less obvious for individual cases. In fact, the specific content you learn from a particular case may seem to have little value for you personally and professionally. But even when cases seem irrelevant, you can still gain experience in understanding and resolving novel situations. It's the *process* of analyzing the situation, more than the situation itself, that generates the learning. The case analyses and case discussions can help develop and refine your abilities for analyzing and resolving difficult situations. And that is good practice for learning to think like a social worker, and for the world of practice.

REFERENCES

Bruner, R. F. (1999). Note to the student: How to study and discuss cases. In *Case studies in finance: Managing for corporate value creation* (3rd ed.; pp. xxiii–xxvi). Boston: Irwin McGraw-Hill. [Also available online at http://faculty.darden.virginia.edu/brunerb/resources_studentnote.htm]

Mauffette-Leenders, L. A., Erskine, J. A., & Leenders, M. R. (1998). *Learning with cases*. London, ONT: Ivey Publishing, Ivey School of Business Administration, The University of Western Ontario.

PART II

Cases

Case 1

Threat to Society?[1]

MACKENZI A. HUYSER

Probation officer Megan Romanowski sat inside Judge Goodman's chambers wondering what choice she possibly had. *I need to just go with what I think is right,* she thought, *but I wonder what my supervisor [Glen Haywood] would say? What if Robert Sanchez turns out to be more of a threat to society than he seems?* She looked up toward the judge as he asked, "What is your recommendation on this issue?"

UNITED STATES PROBATION DEPARTMENT

The United States Probation Department operated under the auspices of the United States District Courts, which functioned as the "trial courts of the federal court system." Congress and the U.S. Constitution mandated that the district courts hear nearly all cases, involving criminal and civil matters, under federal jurisdiction. There were 94 federal districts, including 89 districts in the 50 states

1. This decision case was prepared solely to provide material for class discussion and not to suggest either effective or ineffective handling of the situation depicted. While based on field research regarding an actual situation, names and certain facts may have been disguised to protect confidentiality. The author and editors wish to thank the anonymous case reporter for cooperation in making this account available for the benefit of social work students and instructors. Copyright © 2005 Thomson Learning.

and additional courts in Puerto Rico, the Virgin Islands, Guam, and the Northern Mariana Islands. The United States Probation Department hired federal officers to provide "pretrial services, presentencing services, and/or supervised release services."

Federal officers hired in the supervised release services unit were responsible for a number of activities including but not limited to:

- Conducting investigations on alleged probation violations, supervising release and/or parole violators
- Preparing reports for the court with recommendations for offenders who violated conditions of release
- Supervising persons on probation, parole, and supervised release

Most of the direct contact federal officers had with clients included:

- Maintaining personal contacts with offenders through telephone conversations and office and community visits
- Referring offenders to outside agencies such as medical and drug treatment facilities, employment, and community resources
- Implementing supervision plans
- Providing individual and group counseling
- Evaluating progress toward supervision objectives

Federal officers were required to hold a bachelor's degree from an accredited college or university with specializations in criminal justice, human relations, sociology, or closely related areas. In addition to their education, they were required to attend a minimum of 40 hours of training each year in areas of substance abuse, mental health, policies, and procedures, as well as officer safety and firearms training. Federal officers were required to have a good working knowledge of the systems and relationships of the federal courts.

GLEN HAYWOOD

Glen Haywood, MSW, was the supervised release unit supervisor for the Eastern Michigan District Office. He brought to the position more than 20 years of experience as a federal officer. He had served on the front lines in New York City for nearly 15 years before he moved to the Eastern Michigan District Office and became unit supervisor. Most of his service on the front lines was working with parolees who served time for their involvement in organized crime. The officers who worked with him described his manner as "gruff but friendly."

Glen was responsible for supervising 13 officers in the Eastern Michigan District Office. These federal officers had years of experience and held various degrees, including both bachelor's and master's degrees in social work and criminal justice.

Glen approached supervision with a supportive, but hands-off approach because the officers he supervised had so much experience. He usually played the role of "devil's advocate" when his officers approached him with a difficult decision about a case recommendation. This approach forced his officers to think critically and to explain the reasons behind their recommendations. Because he was so protective of his officers, and occasionally erred on the side of being overprotective, the officers would frequently joke about Glen and his role as the "protective father." Deep down the officers knew, however, he would lay down his life for any one of them.

MEGAN ROMANOWSKI, BSW

Megan Romanowski graduated from a mid-size public university with her BSW at age 22. Fresh out of school she was offered a job at Child Protective Services (CPS) in Wayne County. She had completed her field placement at CPS and liked her supervisor and the people she worked with so much it was an instant "yes" when she was offered a full-time job. She felt her BSW education had trained her well and felt that she had a positive experience in her field placement and was able to handle the job.

At age 25, however, Megan feared having a mental breakdown from work-related stress. She had worked for three-and-a-half years full time at CPS. She frequently shared with family and friends that this job was one of the "most stressful jobs" she ever had. She had grown tired and depressed from the "heart-wrenching" work she was doing. She was "having trouble sleeping" and felt like "my job has taken over my entire life."

Over the course of one month she had to investigate the deaths of three infants. The last of the three was a baby boy Megan had removed from the care of his mother and placed in foster care; he died at the hands of his foster mother within three weeks of her placing him in his temporary home. The emotional trauma of dealing with the deaths of three babies made her feel like she was having a breakdown; she could not function, and knew she had to leave and find a new job. In desperation, she resigned from her position at CPS, effective immediately.

During the next few weeks, Megan thought about the things that drew her to work in the field of social work. For the most part, she enjoyed her work at CPS, the fast-paced work environment, the unexpected calls and immediate action, but working with abused children was too emotionally disturbing.

One week later, a friend told her about an open position for a U.S. probation officer in the Eastern District of Michigan. She thought this position might have some overlapping qualities she enjoyed from her previous experience at CPS, and working with adults might be the kind of change she needed. She applied for the position, was offered the job, and began two weeks later.

MONDAY MORNING, MARCH 11, 2002

On Megan's first day at her new job, she met Kristen, the worker she was replacing. Kristen had been in the position for 10 years and held a master's degree in criminal justice. She had accepted a supervisory role in a different district. Kristen had arranged for Megan to meet most of her caseload in the first week.

"You will have a full caseload of about 70 people," Kristen told Megan.

"That seems quite high," Megan commented, "I think I remember reading that the average was between 55 and 60?" she questioned.

"The average caseload varies depending on if you are in a rural or urban area," Kristen explained. "Because you are in an urban area you are able to see more clients during the month."

That makes sense, Megan thought as she prepared for their afternoon meeting with Robert Sanchez.

"A model parolee," Kristen had said. But as Megan read the file in front of her she couldn't help but question Kristen's statement.

ROBERT SANCHEZ'S STORY

According to his file, Robert Sanchez was born in Puerto Rico in 1958. He moved to St. Louis, Missouri, in 1980, but his file did not explain why. He was currently divorced but had two children from his marriage, a son, age 19, and a daughter, age 13. He had a history of drug use, and his drug of choice was heroin. He admitted that his crimes were committed to support his drug addiction.

In January 1993, Robert Sanchez was arrested in St. Louis for two bank robberies. On both occasions, he walked into a bank with a steel pipe wrapped up in a sweatshirt, said it was a gun, and demanded money from the bank teller. His wife had been in the car, unaware of what he was doing. On both occasions they managed to get away from the bank, but after the second robbery Robert was arrested. In the file, the arresting officer reported he was "high as a kite" when he was picked up two days after the second robbery, and said that Robert had told him that he had spent all of the money he had stolen on heroin. He was taken to the county jail and, the next day, went before a magistrate judge who informed him of the charges and possible sentences. Robert requested bond, but the request was denied because of the violent nature of his crime.

He was held in jail for three months awaiting trial. In April 1993, with the assistance of a court-appointed attorney, he pled guilty, and returned to jail to await his sentencing. On August 21, 1993, he was charged with two counts of bank robbery and sentenced to 92 months in the custody of the Bureau of Prisons to be followed by three years of supervised release. He was immediately transferred to a state prison where he would serve the remainder of his sentence.

In August 1997, Robert was caught smuggling marijuana into prison and was charged with a new felony for possessing contraband. He pled guilty and was sentenced to an additional nine months of prison and three years of supervised release. He was ordered to serve his sentences consecutively and then fulfill his three years of supervised release concurrently.

Prior to his release he filed a pre-release plan and requested relocation to Detroit, Michigan. Kristen had completed the pre-release investigation where she visited the proposed living location and work location, and interviewed all parties with potential contact prior to approving the requested relocation.

The court accepted the placement as appropriate, and Robert Sanchez moved to Detroit, Michigan on September 27, 2001, to serve the remaining three months of his sentence in a halfway house. He had been meeting with Kristen on a weekly basis and, according to the case notes, had been "making excellent progress in adapting to the community." He obtained stable employment in a local restaurant and, according to the notes, his boss "spoke highly of him." His behavior as an inmate in the halfway house was also noted as "excellent." He was subject to drug testing and room searches, and actively participated in counseling and case management services provided in the house.

On December 27, 2001, Kristen approved Robert's move out of the halfway house and into the community. She submitted a supervised release plan that was in the file. Robert and Kristen continued to meet on a weekly basis during his first three months in the community. Kristen noted in the file that Robert "had made a smooth transition in the community" and "was complying with his supervised release plan in all areas."

MONDAY AFTERNOON

Both Kristen and Megan stood up as Robert walked into the office. He was about 5'9" and appeared to weigh about 180 pounds. Megan immediately noticed the numerous tattoos on his arms, neck, and shaved head. Some of the tattoos appeared to be gang tattoos while others scribed "Rebecca" in various shapes and sizes over his exposed skin. *His daughter,* Megan thought, recognizing the name from her review of his file.

"Hi, Robert," Kristen said. "Come on in, I would like you to meet your new probation officer, Megan."

"Hello, Robert, it's nice to meet you," Megan said, extending her hand to shake Robert's.

"It's nice to meet you, too," Robert replied.

"Let's go ahead and have a seat and give Megan an update on your case," Kristen said.

"Well," Robert began slowly, "Things have been going really well. My job is good, I've been getting close to 50 hours a week."

"That's great," Kristen said. "How's your living situation?"

"It's fine," Robert continued. "No changes, I'm still with my brother."

"Good." Kristen turned to Megan. "Robert does a great job of keeping me posted on any changes in his work or living situation."

"Well, if you don't have any questions, Robert, I'll leave you with Megan who will give you her contact information and arrange a next visit. It's been a pleasure working with you, take care," Kristen said.

As Kristen left the room, Megan told Robert she planned to run visits in a similar manner as Kristen and that if he had any questions or needed to give her any information he could call her. Megan provided a business card for Robert and thanked him for coming in and told him she hoped they would have a good working relationship. Robert agreed and shook Megan's hand as he walked out the door. Megan paused before heading to the break room to notify Kristen that she was finished meeting with Robert. She hoped that she had been firm enough with Robert for him to respect her as he had obviously respected Kristen. *We will have to see,* she said to herself as she walked down the hall.

THE FOLLOWING FRIDAY

"Well, I think that's it," Kristen said to Megan, as she gathered the last few items from her desk. "I wish you the best."

The week had been a whirlwind for Megan as she met more than 50 of her 70 clients either by telephone, in-office meetings, or in the community. The rest were notified by mail about Kristen's departure and Kristen said that Megan should just plan on meeting them when their next appointment was scheduled.

Megan thanked Kristen for her time and returned to her office to get organized. It would be a busy weekend of reading numerous client files. Yet she was excited about the position and felt confident she would enjoy the work. There was no doubt it would be challenging, balancing a heavy caseload and time to write numerous reports. But she sensed deep down it would be a good fit for her.

THREE MONTHS LATER

By early June, Megan was starting to feel comfortable in her position. She knew her coworkers and clients fairly well, and had developed a good working relationship with her supervisor, Glen Haywood. She liked how he allowed the officers freedom to make decisions and support when they needed assistance. She had attended additional training on substance abuse and mental health services and she knew the agency policy and procedures book from cover to cover. She no longer felt self-conscious of the loaded firearm she strapped in her holster each time she left the office for a client visit.

She hadn't used her firearm yet, but had come close with Adam, a convicted murderer and sex offender, who was also her new client. He had finished his prison sentence and was serving five years of supervised release. During a routine home visit, Adam snapped at a question she asked him and jumped out of his seat in a threatening manner. Megan stood up and moved toward the door to leave, but not before Adam attempted to push her down. Megan jumped out of the way and pulled out and sprayed her pepper spray. She sprinted out to her car and had only returned to Adam's house with a uniformed police officer accompanying her. This experience had been somewhat of a "reality check" about the importance of her immediate reaction to issues of safety.

TUESDAY, AUGUST 20, 2002

Megan had just returned from getting a cup of coffee from the break room when her telephone rang.

"Officer Romanowski," she answered.

"Megan, this is Robert Sanchez," the voice on the other end of the line said.

"Hi, Robert," Megan replied. "What can I do for you?"

"I am just calling," his voice cracked, "I am just calling to let you know that I was questioned by the police this morning."

"What happened?" Megan asked.

"They were investigating a robbery at the diner," Robert continued, his voice now shaking.

"When did this robbery take place?" Megan asked.

"Last week," Robert answered.

"Were you arrested?" Megan asked.

"No, just questioned," he said quietly.

"Okay . . . well it's good that you called and let me know," Megan continued. "Make sure to keep me posted on any further developments or other contacts you have with the police."

"I will," Robert said.

Megan hung up the telephone and thought for a minute. *Is Robert involved? He was doing so well, he's got stable housing, stable employment, and he quit using drugs. . . . Doesn't he know getting involved in this sort of thing is wrong? He seemed to be listening when we have talked about criminal behavior. . . .*

The ring of her telephone startled Megan back to reality. She composed herself before she answered.

"Officer Romanowski," she said.

"Officer Romanowski, this is Detective Williams from the Detroit Police Department," a male voice said.

"Hello Detective Williams," Megan replied. "How can I help you?"

"I am just calling to notify you that one of your parolees, Robert Sanchez, was just questioned about a robbery that took place on August 15 at Anne's Diner, where he works." Detective Williams continued. "I need to let you know that Robert is considered a suspect in this case."

"Thank you for calling," Megan said. "Please keep me posted on the findings of your investigation."

"I will," Detective Williams replied.

Megan hung up the telephone and stood up. Department policy required that she increase the amount of supervision clients needed if they were involved in any activities that might jeopardize their probation status. She cleared her desk and signed out to check in on Robert at home.

SEPTEMBER 2002

Throughout September, Megan spoke with Detective Williams at least once a week to stay updated on the progress of the investigation. She met once with Robert's boss at work to discuss Robert's employment. She also met with Robert twice a week, once at work and once at home. Even though Robert was a suspect in the case, he remained committed to his job and the goals he had outlined in his supervised release plan. He was tested every week for drug use and remained clean.

The police department continued to investigate the robbery, and it became evident that Robert had been somehow involved in the robbery. The detective had reported that Robert was not directly involved, but had informed the person who had committed the robbery about the cash box and where it was located in the restaurant.

On Friday, September 20, Robert called Megan and informed her that he had just received notice that he needed to appear in court in four days to be arrested for his involvement in the robbery. Immediately following this information, Robert's boss had fired him. Robert was very upset about being fired. Megan asked for details about his court date and told him she would see him in court. As soon as Megan hung up the phone, she got up and walked two doors down to her supervisor's office. She had an open and honest relationship with her supervisor; everything was "laid out in the open" with him. Glen was sitting at his desk and looked up as Megan knocked and quickly walked into his office.

"What's up?" Glen asked.

"I just got off the phone with Robert Sanchez," Megan began. "He's going to be arrested for a role in this robbery at the restaurant."

"Get a warrant for his arrest and send him back to prison for violating parole," Glen replied immediately.

"I don't know," Megan began, assuming Glen was playing the devil's advocate role. "He's had a huge decrease in his criminal thinking. He's made great progress.

He's not testing positive for drug use, he's in a stable housing environment, and up to this point has had stable employment. He's taken ten steps forward. I don't want to put him all the way back to step one," Megan continued. "He will be punished for this crime by the state, let's see what they do before we jump in and punish him as well. What if we could get a warrant for his arrest, but recommend that he return to the halfway house? This way he can continue to make progress."

"He is an armed bank robber who violated his parole by committing another robbery," Glen said firmly and in a serious tone. "Lock him up."

Megan stood up and returned to her office. She could tell that Glen was serious and he wanted Robert locked up. She had so many questions: *Was the reasoning I presented to Glen not good enough? Robert has been so honest and up front about the situation and he was making so much progress—this has to be worth giving him more options than just being sent back to prison!*

TUESDAY, SEPTEMBER 24, 2002

Megan was called into Judge Goodman's chambers prior to Robert Sanchez's arraignment. She wondered what choice she possibly had. *I need to just go with what I think is right,* she thought, but in her head she wondered what Glen would say. *What if Robert Sanchez is more of a threat to society than he seems?* She looked up toward the judge as he asked, "What is your recommendation on this issue?"

Case 2

Twice a Victim. . . .
In English, Please[1]

HELEN HARRIS

I t was unusually cold in Abilene, Texas, in November 2001. The West Texas
wind was blowing and chilling. Albert Mendoza was beginning to feel a part
of the Crime Victims Center, the agency he had been assigned to as a baccalaureate social work intern. He was pleased that his Spanish-speaking skills
were valued in the agency and that his social work skills were improving. But
as he sat across from Carlos Hernandez waiting for his response, Albert felt his
anxiety growing. *Establishing trust and asking hard questions is so much more complicated for me in Spanish. And now that I have asked him about his social security
card, what will I do with the answer? What if he's not here legally?*

THE CRIME VICTIMS CENTER

The Crime Victims Center, in downtown Abilene, was established initially as a
rape crisis center and evolved over the years into an umbrella agency providing
comprehensive services to victims of crime. Funded largely by public and

1. This decision case was prepared solely to provide material for class discussion and not to
suggest either effective or ineffective handling of the situation depicted. While based on field
research regarding an actual situation, names and certain facts may have been disguised to
protect confidentiality. The author and editors wish to thank the anonymous case reporter for
cooperation in making this account available for the benefit of social work students and
instructors. Copyright © 2005 Thomson Learning.

foundation grants, the center included a children's counseling program, a children's advocacy program, and an adult victim's program. Six social workers, a community educator, and support staff worked together to provide individual and group counseling to victims of crime in the city and surrounding counties.

The adult victims program's service delivery structure included hotline services for domestic violence and sexual assault. Hotline volunteers answered the crisis line and supported clients at the hospital during initial questioning and examination. Intake workers at the agency were responsible for describing to clients the services of the agency, initial assessment of the incident and request for services, psychosocial assessment, and assignment to a counselor. The agency's mission—to serve victims of crime—included helping victims feel safe from perpetrators. No perpetrators were seen as clients at the agency and perpetrators were barred from the property. The agency had to be accessed through a locked front door with a buzzer release system operated by agency staff. The sign above the buzzer read: "Please ring for entrance." Albert noted that the sign was in English.

Services at the agency were driven by the agency structure and funding sources. Most of the agency's clinical staff were masters-level social workers or licensed professional counselors. One BSW worker did case management services in a counselor role. The center was the recipient of United Way and other grant funds, allowing it to serve clients regardless of the client's ability to pay. The administrative team had developed a strong working relationship with area law enforcement; moreover, they were able to coordinate the delivery of services and criminal justice advocacy for victims of crimes. The agency frequently received referrals for counseling from law enforcement personnel.

ALBERT MENDOZA

Albert Mendoza's personal strengths as a social work intern included his maternal Scotch-Irish heritage and his paternal Mexican American heritage. His parents had raised him in San Antonio, near his father's family. The Mendoza family had lived in the United States for three generations and Albert's father made sure his wife and sons had weekly contact with his extended family. Albert's mother, a teacher from Alabama, was the epicenter of Albert's nuclear family, but did not have much contact with her own extended family in Alabama. Albert remembered feeling he was growing up with two cultures: he learned about being "white" from his mother while also taking pride in the Mendoza family roots in San Antonio.

The Mendoza extended family was made up of all native Spanish speakers and Albert would sometimes get lost in the conversations at large family gatherings. His cousins were adept at "code switching," or alternating languages and using "Spanglish," a combination of English and Spanish languages. Albert remembered his grandfather saying in exasperation: "You young people are losing the language. No Spanglish!" Albert also experienced the feeling that he was "looked down on" by whites for his Latino heritage and that Latinos distrusted him because of his Euro-American heritage. Not only was Albert not "100%" fluent in Spanish but his language skills were limited to his childhood experiences with the Mendoza family. The more intimate and developmentally important conversations that generally happen in the nuclear family all happened in English for Albert.

During his middle school years, Albert experienced firsthand the challenges of family disruption and family violence. He watched his parents struggle with their relationship and their cross-cultural marriage. Their differences increased, and finally Albert's parents argued and eventually fought. Albert saw his father grow increasing resentful of his wife's leadership in the home and watched the violence escalate as he experienced firsthand the pain of cyclical family violence and reconciliation. One terrible night, he helped his mother pack and they went to a family abuse shelter. There were several separations before his parents divorced. Albert lived with the ambivalence of loving his parents and resenting their frailties. He knew, even as a very young man, that he would someday work to help children and families with the struggles of poverty, of culture clashes, and of power struggles in families. He first considered being a social worker as a teen when he was staying in a family shelter. He determined then: *Someday I will help families deal with the kind of stuff my family is going through.* He became immersed in the punk rock subculture, finding there others who shared his disdain for inequality and injustice and who shared his determination to "make it happen." He would not be one to complain about what had happened to him and to his family. *I will act; I will make a difference!*

After high school, Albert knew he needed a college education in order to really help families with the challenges of pain and violence. One of the social workers at the Family Violence Shelter encouraged him to consider a social work career, and that would mean at least four years of college. He struggled with his decision about where to go to school. There were several strong social work programs in and around San Antonio. Ready for greater independence, Albert decided to stay in Texas but to move away from home. In Abilene, a moderately sized town, there was a Baptist university known for being conservative and socially conscious at the same time. Albert knew that his blue hair and punk rock style of dress would challenge the system there, and he looked forward to making his own place in the world. Albert packed his Honda Civic with all of his possessions, including his Mendoza family album and genealogy. On campus, he joined the Hispanic Student Association and the social work student organization, got a part-time job waiting tables to help pay expenses, and dove into his studies. The course work included sections on cultural diversity and ethnic sensitive practice. Albert's growing self-awareness included the realization that his bicultural experience had provided him with some understanding of each culture, but Albert realized more and more that he had a full understanding of neither. Even more startling was his Spanish class experience. He discovered that he was fluent in Spanish at only the third- or fourth-grade level. His visits with family as a college student felt like forays into the Mendoza extended family experience that often resulted in him feeling somehow left out. He remembered the teasing of his cousins: "Just give White Boy some Tex–Mex food and he'll be happy."

EDUCATION: MOVING
FROM KNOWING TO DOING

The social work curriculum included several opportunities to volunteer in area agencies. One agency, the Crime Victims Center, enjoyed a strong reputation among the students for providing good services, serving clients who had no financial means to pay, and allowing students to do significant hands-on work. Albert decided to become more familiar with the agency and completed the 30-hour training for working the crisis hotline. The training reminded him of his own troubled youth. He made an appointment with Mrs. Wilson, his faculty advisor, and discussed his growing passion to work with Hispanic families in crisis.

"I just believe that my experiences with family violence and all that I'm learning in my classes is helping me figure out how to help other families in the same situation."

Mrs. Wilson recommended, "Why don't you focus your writing in your assignments on the issue of family violence? You have the opportunity to understand several cultures and to help your clients identify the strengths in each."

Albert followed her advice and wrote several assignments about his experiences with family violence and how much social work intervention had helped him process that and use it as a strength in defining his professional goals. During his junior year, he called Dr. Soto, the field coordinator, and went by to visit about his upcoming field internship.

"I think I would like to work with Hispanic families," Albert explained. "And I'm ready to work with families in crisis."

"Well, the Crime Victims Center is requesting a Spanish-speaking intern," Dr. Soto responded. "They have no Spanish-speaking staff and are increasingly confronted with the need for translation and services in Spanish."

"Sure! I'd like to be placed there. But," Albert hesitated, "I want to work with clients as a social worker, not just a translator."

"Yes, of course, that's a good point. I believe you will be doing intakes and psychosocial assessments for the agency and will, with time, be assigned cases in the counseling program. In fact, I'll call them tomorrow to clarify your role as a social work intern and discuss assigning clients who are Spanish speaking to you for case management."

"That is super," Albert replied. "I'm sure, then, that my choice for internship is the Crime Victims Center."

THE COMPLEXITIES OF HELPING

After his interview with Susan McFarland, the Crime Victims Center field instructor, Albert called Dr. Soto, the field director, excitedly: "This is going to be such a good placement for me. They don't have any Spanish-speaking counselors among the full-time staff, but they have contracted with a Spanish-speaking counselor from the community to help out. And the best thing is the chance to work as part of a multidisciplinary team. They work with Child Protective Services, with the police department and the district attorney's office. It's all pretty exciting! And it looks like I'll see clients in the intake and case management services who speak little or no English."

The first two months of the placement sped by. Albert attended classes at the university on Mondays, Wednesdays, and Thursdays. Those days, he wore jeans, sported spiked blue hair, and enjoyed the easy camaraderie of college life. On Tuesdays and Fridays, he dressed in khakis, sprayed his hair black, and worked as a social work intern at the center. Albert reported in his field seminar that he saw an average of four clients a day for intakes, had begun working with a group of sexually abused middle school boys, and participated in staffings and group supervision each week. He was busy at the agency and was called on at least twice a week to translate for Spanish-speaking clients or their family members.

One Friday in November, Albert checked his message box and found a message from a social worker at the local hospital. The center's receptionist had recorded the message: "Hispanic male treated for injuries and released at the hospital last night. Hospital SW referred to the center for assault. Difficulty communicating with client—spoke almost no English—but housekeeper translated. Center appt. at 3 PM."

Shortly before 3 PM, the buzzer at the front desk rang. Albert had decided to wait at the front desk for his new client and answered the buzzer in English and in Spanish: "May I help you? *¿Le puedo ayudar?*"

"*Soy Carlos Hernandez. El del hospital* (I am Carlos Hernandez. From the hospital)," a man responded quickly.

"*Sigue.* (Come on in.)" Albert buzzed the door open and Carlos walked in with a woman and a young girl with wide, frightened eyes. To Albert, Carlos appeared to be in his late 30s, with a medium build, and dark hair and eyes. His head was bandaged, his cheek and eye were blackened, his left arm was in a sling, and he walked gingerly.

Albert held out his hand to Carlos, introduced himself in Spanish, and invited Carlos to come to his office. Albert looked at the woman, smiled, and spoke softly to her in Spanish.

"*Voy a hablar con tu esposo en mi oficina. ¿Puedes esperar en la sala de esperar con tu hija? Es posible que tu hija le gustaria juegar con los juegetes en la sala de esperar.* (Your husband and I will be talking in my office. Would you and your daughter wait here in the waiting room? Your daughter might enjoy playing with the toys in the waiting room.)"

The woman smiled softly and said "thank you," with a noticeable Spanish accent.

"*¿Hablas inglés?* (Do you speak English?)," Albert asked.

"Only a little," she said and quickly translated for Carlos.

As they entered Albert's office, Albert indicated with his hand for Carlos to have a seat. Carlos met his eyes squarely and remained standing. Albert stood with him and began to explain the agency services in Spanish. He briefly described the intake process and the counseling services for Carlos.

But Carlos interrupted, "*Pero necesito dinero para pagar al hospital. Y mi esposa y mi hija, tienen miedo. Necesito ayuda para ellas.* (But I need money to pay for the hospital bill. And my wife and my daughter . . . they are scared. I need help for them.)"

Though able to understand Carlos, Albert's mind began to race. *Oh, man! I know what I want to say but my Spanish isn't good enough to explain what benefits he's eligible for. Hmmm . . . what do I say?* Albert searched for words to explain that there might be help available but he would need more information from Carlos.

"*Por favor siéntese. Explícame lo que pasó.* (Please sit. Tell me what happened.)"

Carlos sat down heavily and began to tell his story. As Carlos talked, Albert's head was spinning: *I feel so inadequate right now. I wonder if he's frustrated by my poor Spanish. I hope he isn't worried that I can't help him? Will he get frustrated with my Spanish and bolt from the room?*

As best Albert could understand, Carlos Hernandez and his family had been the victims of random violence the previous night. They were in their home late in the evening when they heard banging on the front door. As Carlos reached the front room, the door burst open and an African American man pushed into the room pointing a gun at him. He shouted at Carlos in English but Carlos wasn't able to understand him. Mrs. Hernandez rushed to the front room, followed by their daughter, Rocio. The two arrived as the intruder shot Mr. Hernandez twice, kicked him in the head, and ran back out of the house. One bullet had grazed Carlos's head and the other passed through his shoulder. The family was stunned and terrified. "*Porque esto nos está pasando?* (Oh no. Oh no. Why is this happening to us?)" Mrs. Hernandez called 911 for an ambulance. She and Rocio rode with him in the ambulance to the hospital where Mr. Hernandez had surgery and was kept overnight and released the next day. A police officer spoke to them in broken Spanish. Finally, the hospital social worker asked a housekeeper to translate, and the Hernandez family was able to explain that they did not know the assailant and did not know why he had broken into their home.

At this point, Carlos looked up bitterly, stating, "*El seguía preguntando por drogas.* (The man kept asking about drugs.)" Carlos continued, "*Nosotros no tenemos drogas. No se lo que quería* (We don't have drugs. I don't know what he wanted.)"

"*Debe ser difícil* (It must be hard)," Albert answered gently. Carlos answered with resignation: "*Solamente necesito dinero para pagar por el hospital. Y necesito más cirugía.* (I just need money to pay for the hospital, and I need more surgery.)"

In Spanish, Albert explained about the Crime Victim's Compensation Fund and told Carlos that he believed the bills could be covered by the fund. He told him the requirement that Carlos must cooperate fully as the police investigated the assault.

Carlos asked quietly, "*¿Y mi familia? ¿Que pasaran con ellas?* (What about my family?)" He reported that his daughter had nightmares when she tried to sleep following the incident.

Albert assured Carlos that his family would be eligible for counseling as crime victims since they observed the assault. He also told Carlos they would be referred to the Spanish-speaking therapist in the community for counseling services.

MISCUE

Late the following Thursday, Susan McFarland telephoned Albert at his home. "Albert, sorry to call you at home." Albert wondered what could be wrong but answered: "No problem. What's up?" Susan explained: "Carlos came by the agency this afternoon. He was agitated and upset and asked repeatedly for you. Carlos tried to show the case manager at the front desk a medical bill and kept saying something in Spanish. We couldn't understand him so we got him to write it down for you. He wrote: *"Albert me dijo que el doctor iba ser pagado."*

"Oh," Albert translated, "that means 'Albert told me the doctor would be paid.'"

"Anyhow, we tried to explain that you were only in the agency on Tuesdays and Fridays. In fact, the case manager asked Carlos to come back the next day and to bring his social security card when he returned. Finally, he nodded and left. We think he understood us."

Albert nodded slowly. "I've been thinking about this all afternoon. I'm worried that I can't help Carlos and his family," Albert responded. "I might even make things worse for them. My Spanish isn't always that good and I don't have much experience."

"You're doing fine," Susan responded. "We are glad you are here for them."

Albert wondered to himself, *I sure hope so. Could this case get even more complicated? Is there more to this story?*

When Carlos returned the next day, Albert explained that he was only in the agency Tuesdays and Fridays and asked whether the family had seen a counselor.

Carlos said they had made an appointment, but he was concerned about appointments because he could not afford the bills. Albert reassured him again that the expenses should be covered under Crime Victims Compensation (CVC).

"*Carlos, necesito la tarjeta de seguridad social para llamar el numero.* (Carlos, I need to see your social security card so I can call in the number.)"

"*Listo te lo traigo la proxima semana* (OK. I can bring it next week.)"

I wonder how much he understands, Carlos wondered. *I hope I'm right that CVC will pay this bill.*

"Do you want me to call the medical provider in the meantime and clarify with them that you are applying for CVC?"

Albert explained the application and approval process. "I would like for you to sign an informed consent form," Albert explained in Spanish. "This will allow me to communicate with the medical providers and with CVC." The form was in English, and Albert translated the technical language as best he could. Carlos signed the form and left the office.

Albert sat down frustrated. His questions persisted and grew. *What does he understand?* But a new, more basic question was beginning to trouble him: *What if Carlos isn't in the country legally? What if he doesn't have a social security card? How do I advocate for him? How do I make sure I don't disclose information that leads to his deportation? How do I bring this up without scaring him more?*

Albert's mind began to race: *What are my responsibilities as a social worker? As an intern? To the agency? To the client? To the university? Should I have thought of this earlier? Did my lack of proficiency in Spanish contribute to this situation? Why doesn't an agency that provides services to so many Spanish-speaking clients provide a Spanish-speaking staff member?* Albert had spent two months at the agency feeling that his skills were an asset to the agency. Suddenly, he felt an incredible, even overwhelming responsibility for the situation. Albert would have to talk with Susan about the center's policy regarding illegal immigrants. But that could mean Carlos and his family would be deported. On the other hand, not telling could put the agency and his supervisor in jeopardy. Carlos needed help now. Albert wondered, *What do I do next?*

Case 3

I Can't Find Her!¹

SUSAN MURTY

"**I** can't find her!" Jim Snyder repeated, sounding scared and helpless. "She's gone again!"

Social worker Emelia Brown, from the Senior Services Center, stood in the tiny kitchen of the Snyder's mobile home, trying to grasp the situation. It was a chilly windy Friday afternoon, the last day of November 2002.

"What should I do?" the frail 78-year-old implored, wringing his hands. "I can't find her!"

Feeling the panic in Mr. Snyder's voice, Emelia feared losing control. *What can I do?* she asked herself silently. *What should I do?*

SENIOR SERVICES CENTER

The Senior Services Center, located in Centerville, Iowa, was a nonprofit agency designed to enhance the well-being of seniors living in Hunter County. Founded by local residents in 1968, it provided support, recreational activities, and educational opportunities to people over 55 years of age.

---

1. This decision case was prepared solely to provide material for class discussion and not to suggest either effective or ineffective handling of the situation depicted. While based on field research regarding an actual situation, names and certain facts may have been disguised to protect confidentiality. The author and editors wish to thank the anonymous case reporter for cooperation in making this account available for the benefit of social work students and instructors. Copyright © 2005 Thomson Learning.

The clients of the Senior Services Center lived in their own homes or in subsidized housing and were 55 years old and older. Many came into the center for congregate meals and activities. The Meals on Wheels program was one of the first programs at the senior center. At first it was run entirely by volunteers, but by the 1980s a staff of three professionals oversaw the program.

Although the center was originally funded by local contributions, since 1980 the agency had received most of its funding from the Area Agency on Aging that served the two county area surrounding Centerville. In 1998, a new program, the Frail Elderly Case Management program, was initiated with funds provided by the Older Americans Act. This case management program was designed to help older people receive services so they could stay in their own homes rather than be placed in a nursing home.

The staff at the Senior Services Center had various levels of training. The director, Jim Armstrong, had a PhD in psychology. The social services coordinator, Sara Greene, MSW, had extensive experience working with the elderly. Before coming to work at the Senior Services Center in 1994, she had been a gerontological social worker at a mental health center in the Quad Cities, a metropolitan area in eastern Iowa. Other staff members included a nurse, Jill Richards, RN, and the activities coordinator, Mary Ann Stewart, who had a bachelor's degree in English. Several part-time staff members led center activities, and dedicated volunteers assisted with activities at the center and with Meals on Wheels.

THE NEW SOCIAL WORKER

Twenty-two-year-old Emelia Brown graduated with her BA degree in social work from the University of Iowa in May 2001. All through college she worked a part-time evening shift at a home for the developmentally disabled. Since graduation, she had been working at the Senior Services Center as volunteer coordinator in Centerville, not far from her own hometown of Granby.

Emelia's chief responsibility was to supervise the Meals on Wheels program. She was responsible for determining eligibility for the program and for filing the required reports. In addition, she assisted other staff with activities at the senior center and with special events and projects. Under supervision from Sara Greene, she responded to special needs and crisis situations among the elders served at the center.

Emelia worked most closely with three staff members: Jim Armstrong, Sara Greene, and Mary Ann Stewart. She met with them in an interdisciplinary team called the "case review team." Emelia presented the Meals on Wheels cases for review each month on a schedule so that each client was reviewed every six months.

This was Emelia's first professional job as a social worker and she loved it. Her first day on the job, Mrs. Greene made a point of telling her, "I am so glad to have another social worker on staff here!" Emelia assisted other staff with a variety of senior center activities and soon got to know many of the seniors personally. *I have become their favorite,* she sometimes smiled to herself. *They always tell me I have so much energy and enthusiasm.* While visiting her hometown, she told friends, "I am so glad I can do something useful in my job!" After six months, Emelia felt things were going pretty well with her job. *I want so much for Mrs. Greene to think well of me,* she said to herself. *I hope I won't make any mistakes or get into any trouble over my work.*

EMELIA'S WORK AT THE CENTER

Although she helped with other activities at the center, Emelia's favorite program was Meals on Wheels. She felt it reached the elders who had the greatest needs. They were all age 70 or older and had a difficult time getting around their homes. Some were quite disabled and homebound. Nevertheless, she could tell they were proud of their independence. Many told Emelia how much they wanted to stay in their own homes. "I've always taken care of myself," one of them said during a recent visit, "and I don't intend to stop now!"

When she started her new job, Emelia was pleased to learn that there was a group of 15 volunteers who had been delivering the meals. Many of them had been doing it for years. *What a loyal and faithful group of volunteers they are,* Emelia soon concluded, *what a good team they make! They usually arrive early to pick up the meals at the nursing home. They're very dependable. All I have to do is make sure that they knew where to go and what meal to take to whom.* That was important because some of the elders had special diets. But there had never been a problem with any of the volunteers. The only thing Emelia had to worry about was reminding the volunteers to fill out their paperwork.

And there were also lots of forms and paperwork that Emelia had to fill out herself. It kept her quite busy. But every now and then, when a volunteer called in sick or was out of town, Emelia got to fill in and deliver the meals herself.

"That's my favorite part of the job," she told her friend, Brooke Winchester. "You can tell it means a lot to them when we bring a hot meal. And I'm really pretty good at listening to them and their stories. I can always make them smile!" She continued, "You know, this is why I went into social work! I know I'm making a difference!" Emelia was sure her professors in the social work program would be proud of her, if they could see her in the new job.

A SWEET COUPLE

Emelia first met Jim and Zelda Snyder two months after starting work, when she visited their home to do a biannual reassessment for the Meals on Wheels program. *They are such a sweet couple,* she thought on her first visit. They told Emelia they had been married almost 50 years.

When Emelia first visited them in their mobile home, she had a nice long talk with Mrs. Snyder. She was a delightful person and seemed to be functioning well at age 75 in spite of her arthritis. Emelia could tell she was proud of their little mobile home, although they had lived on a big farm for many years.

"This mobile home is a lot less work to clean than that old farmhouse ever was!" she said. But Mrs. Snyder worried that her husband missed the farm. "He used to get up early every morning and go out and take care of the animals and the crops," she said. "He doesn't quite know what to do with himself now."

"Would you like to continue to get the home-delivered meals?" Emelia asked.

"Yes, honey, I think so. There are days I just can't seem to keep up and it sure is nice to have those meals. It's good for Jim to have a good dinner. And I don't get around so good any more with this arthritis. It keeps getting worse and really slows me down. That new medicine I am taking does not seem to help. So, if you can put us down for those meals again, we sure would appreciate it!"

"Does getting these meals," Emelia made sure to ask, "help you stay at home and live independently?"

"Oh, yes," Mrs. Snyder answered. "Jim doesn't know how to cook. We'd have to move to a home if we didn't get these meals!"

Emelia completed the assessment form and left feeling good about her visit with the Snyders. "I really do love this job," she said aloud to herself as she pulled out of the driveway.

THE CASE REVIEW TEAM

When Emelia reported on the Snyders at the regular case review meeting at the end of August, she was brief:

"The Snyders are still receiving home-delivered meals. They are doing well and maintaining their independence. I recommend that the meals continue. "How is their health?" asked Sara Greene. "Did you notice any health problems that would concern you?"

"Well, no, nothing concerned me," Emelia replied. "And I haven't had any calls from the volunteers that say there is a problem with anything so I am assuming there are no changes. The Snyders told me in the assessment earlier this month that the meals help them to remain independent at home. They are really a sweet couple and they need the meals, so I am asking the team to approve the continuation of meals."

After the brief report, the team approved the home-delivered meals on Emelia's recommendation and went on to discuss other cases.

THE CRISIS

On Friday, November 30, 2002, Emelia came in to work early, planning to complete the paperwork for the Meals on Wheels program for the month. The report had to be done and on the director's desk by 5 PM. However, just as she arrived, the phone rang.

"I'm really not feeling well!" It was Leticia Van Husen, one of her most faithful volunteers. "I think I might be coming down with the flu. I have a headache and I feel achy and real tired. I hate to disappoint my folks. But I don't want to give them the flu. What do you think I should do?"

"Don't you worry," Emelia reassured her, "you take care of yourself. I can fill in for you. I have the list right here. You just go to bed and have a good rest!"

Actually, Emelia enjoyed leaving her desk for a while and seeing the seniors on the Meals on Wheels route. It had been more than three months since she had completed all of her home visits and assessments in August.

Later that morning, Emelia picked up the hot meals at the nursing home and packed them in the insulated carriers. After making sure that diabetic meals had been provided for Mr. Snyder and Mrs. Swanson, she loaded everything into her car and started out to deliver the meals. She stopped at Mrs. Jones's house, and went on to Mr. Laverson, who kept her talking about some leaks in his roof that he wanted to have fixed. Next, she arrived at the Snyders' home. Mr. Snyder came outside before she had even parked the car. She was struck by how thin he looked. He started talking to her through the car window.

"I don't know what to do! She has never been gone this long before. She usually just hides in the bushes in the backyard. I don't know what to do!" He started to cry. "Where could she have gone this time?"

Emelia asked if they could go inside to talk, and Mr. Snyder nodded. Emelia grabbed their two meals out of the backseat and followed him into the kitchen of the little mobile home.

There she stood, with the meals in their insulated carriers, looking for a place to put them down. And there was Mr. Snyder, so upset he was barely able to talk.

I can't find her!" he repeated. "What should I do?"

Emelia's thoughts were racing. *This could be serious. And it sounds like this has happened before. How could that be? Why didn't he tell the volunteers about this so we would know what was going on? Or maybe he did tell them! Did they know? Could it be that they thought it was not important enough to report to me?*

Emelia needed to gather her thoughts, because she knew the first thing to do was to make sure Mrs. Snyder was all right. Emelia had so many questions: *How long had she been gone? Could she have wandered over to the busy street near by? Could she have been hit by a car? It's getting pretty cold out there. Did she have a coat and mittens on? There was some snow and ice on the sidewalks. What if she slipped and fell?*

Emelia shoved some things aside on the kitchen counter and put down the meal carriers. She took a deep breath. Then she said, "Mr. Snyder, I know you are worried about your wife. Why don't you come over here and sit down so we can talk for a minute?"

Emelia led him into the living room and got him to sit down in an easy chair. "Do you have any idea where she is?" Emelia asked, trying to sound calm.

Mr. Snyder stared at her, looking bewildered. "I've got to find her! What should I do?" he kept repeating over and over.

"Just tell me all about it," said Emelia, reaching out to take his hand.

I am pretty worried about him, Emelia thought to herself. *He's so anxious, and not too steady on his feet. Maybe I should get some other people to come over here to help us look for Mrs. Snyder. But I don't want to leave him alone.*

Emelia tried to think about who else she could call at the Senior Services Center to come to the house and help her. Panic began to rise and her breathing felt tight. *What am I going to do? What if something has happened to Mrs. Snyder? I hope she's OK!*

Emelia pulled herself back from these racing thoughts to repeat her questions to Mr. Snyder. "Tell me what happened. When did she leave?"

"It was about an hour ago or so. I was in the bathroom. When I came out, I noticed that the front door was open. I looked for Zelda and she wasn't anywhere inside. So then I went out and called for her, but she didn't come. I went to all her normal hiding spots in our yard and the neighbors' yard, but she wasn't there. Then I remembered someone was coming over with the meals. I was hoping you could help."

"I'm glad I'm here to help," Emelia said. "This must be frightening for you. It's hard to deal with something like this on your own."

"I'm so scared!" Mr. Snyder acknowledged. "What if she wanders over to the main road? She could get hit by a car!"

Emelia felt scared, too. She decided she better talk to her supervisor. She pulled out her cell phone to call Mrs. Greene at the Senior Services Center. She was disappointed to get the voice-mail message: "Mrs. Greene is not available, please leave a message." Emelia left a message to call her back as soon as possible.

When she looked up, Emelia saw that Mr. Snyder was standing up again. He seemed very agitated.

"Come over here and sit down next to me, and take a deep breath for a moment," Emelia said, patting the sofa beside her.

Mr. Snyder sat down beside Emelia. He kept repeating "Where is she? What should I do?"

HOW SERIOUS IS THIS?

Emelia tried to appear calm but her mind continued to race. *Maybe the Snyders shouldn't be living on their own any more. It's beginning to look as if they can't handle things. How serious is this?*

Maybe when everything settles down, I should talk to them about moving to a facility where they would have someone to look after them, some place where there would be some supervision and monitoring. There are the subsidized living apartments over on Elm Street. They are pretty nice.

Emelia asked Mr. Snyder again to tell her more about what happened, but he could only respond with the question, " What should I do" over and over again.

"I know you are worried" Emelia said softly. "We will see what we can do as soon as I get a call back from the center."

Mr. Snyder doesn't look like he could handle any difficult decisions right now, thought Emelia. *Should I recommend that they move to somewhere safer? What if they don't want to go? What if they get mad at me?*

Five minutes had passed and Mrs. Greene still had not called. Emelia started to feel panicked. *Maybe this is all my fault,* thought Emelia. *Maybe I've let the volunteers do too much on their own. They seemed to know what they were doing. They had been delivering meals to these folks for years, long before I started working here. Maybe I haven't monitored them closely enough.*

"Don't worry, Mr. Snyder," Emelia said, reaching out to take his hand. "Everything is going to be all right!" Then, she rubbed her forehead. She felt tension building up in her neck, too. *Maybe I'm not cut out for social work after all. I like my work, but this is more than I bargained for!* Emelia felt her head spinning.

And what about the report that's due by 5 PM? she wondered. *Mrs. Greene has said again and again* how important it is *to get those reports turned in on time, but surely it's more important to make sure Mrs. Snyder is OK right now.*

Meanwhile, Mr. Snyder was still murmuring, "I've got to find her. What should I do?"

Emelia looked at her watch. More than 15 minutes had passed since she arrived at the Snyders' home. Mrs. Greene had not called back. *I can't wait any longer. I have to take some steps to find Mrs. Snyder and make sure Mr. Snyder stays safe, too.*

Case 4

I Need to Advocate for My Client![1]

PATRICIA GLEASON-WYNN

Though steaming inside, social work intern Celia O'Neill sat quietly at the south nurses' station at Country Acres thinking about what had just happened. *I can't believe this! They talked about my client like he wasn't there . . . but he was there and he could hear them! This is the last straw . . . . I've got to do something!*

COUNTRY ACRES NURSING HOME

Country Acres Nursing Home was located in Wilson, Texas, a rural community one hour's drive from Austin. Wilson's 30,000 citizens included a mix of long time rural residents and professionals who worked in Austin but returned to Wilson each evening for the peacefulness of a "bedroom community" that still retained a rural feeling.

Country Acres was a 129-bed private nonprofit nursing facility. In operation since 1975, it offered long-term care and services including rehabilitation services consisting of physical, occupational, and speech therapies.

1. This decision case was prepared solely to provide material for class discussion and not to suggest either effective or ineffective handling of the situation depicted. While based on field research regarding an actual situation, names and certain facts may have been disguised to protect confidentiality. The author and editors wish to thank the anonymous case reporter for cooperation in making this account available for the benefit of social work students and instructors. Copyright © 2005 Thomson Learning.

Jeffrey Allen, the administrator, oversaw the entire nursing home operation. Connie Bell, RN, Director of Nursing, supervised the 14 nurses and 28 nurse aides. Betty Williams, LSW (Licensed Social Worker), Director of Social Services, ensured that the resident's medically related psychosocial needs were met, Celia O'Neill, Activity Director, developed and provided, either directly or through volunteer help, activities to meet the needs and interests of the nursing home residents such as exercise programs, religious programs, games, and other intellectual stimulation. Her part-time assistant, Beth Smith, assisted Celia in planning and providing the activities, and oversaw the activity department in Celia's absence. The facility staff also included the business manager, Tina Gonzalez, and her administrative assistant in the business office, five kitchen aides, three housekeeping workers, and two maintenance workers.

Many of the residents admitted to Country Acres were old, frail, and dependent and while a few residents returned home, many had no plans for leaving the facility. A few clients paid directly for services; however, most clients applied for Medicaid assistance, which they could only receive if they qualified medically and financially.

Guidelines for Medicaid were very specific and detailed. The Director of Nursing determined medical eligibility of applicants, and caseworkers from the Department of Human Services (DHS) determined financial eligibility of applicants. Medicaid's Vendor Payment program made payments directly to providers such as Country Acres. Program guidelines required that providers accept the Medicaid reimbursement level as payment in full. According to the Texas Medicaid requirements, eligible clients had to be residents requiring nursing care. Those in a nursing facility had to have lived 30 consecutive days in the facility to be eligible.

DHS income criteria required that applicants have an income no greater than $1,692 per month for an individual or $3,384 for a couple. Also, the applicant could have "countable resources" of no more than $2,000 for an individual or $3,000 for a couple (if both spouses were applying). These included bank accounts, stocks, bonds, and cash-value life insurance policies.

SOCIAL WORK SERVICES

Two social workers brought their professional experience to Country Acres. Betty Williams, the Director of Social Services, had a BSW and five years of practice experience in hospital and hospice settings, but she had only been working at Country Acres for two months. As the Director of Social Services, she was responsible for providing to the 129 residents medically related social services that were designed to improve or maintain each resident's ability to control everyday physical, mental, emotional, spiritual, and psychosocial needs. Betty also assisted in coordinating community resources to help the facility meet the needs of its resident and families and she was a valuable member of the interdisciplinary care team.

Sally Jones, a contract social work consultant, had been providing social work consultation to Country Acres on and off for the past eight years. Sally was a licensed clinical social worker (LCSW) with more than 20 years of nursing home experience. At the request of the administrator, Sally continued to provide support and guidance to Betty as she learned to deal with the demands of a new job.

CELIA O'NEILL, SOCIAL WORK INTERN

Celia O'Neill felt excited about beginning her social work internship at Country Acres Nursing Home, especially because she enjoyed working with older people in her role as activity director. She was a member of the Austin State University (ASU) class of 2002 and graduation was just two semesters away. Celia was looking forward to finishing her degree, getting licensed, and starting her first job as a real social worker. At age 39, it seemed she had been going to school forever; she had been enrolled part time at Austin State and commuted two days a week from Wilson to the city for classes. During the past year, Celia's husband Pete lost his job, which made things tough financially at home. But soon her schooling would be complete and she would be able to earn a full-time salary as a social worker.

Working in social services was not a new experience for Celia. Prior to employment at Country Acres, Celia worked for two years as the director of Sanctuary House, a mental health and mental retardation home for adults. For the past 12 years she had been Country Acres' certified activity director. For the most part she enjoyed her job, but recently she had become frustrated with some of the nursing staff and the negative comments that they made about the residents. For example, about two years ago, she overheard a nurse say to a resident, "Stop bugging me, I will get your medicine to you when I get around to it." Celia was horrified with what she heard, and immediately reported it to Connie Bell, assuming that she would be outraged and reprimand the employee. Much to Celia's surprise, Connie said, "You probably misheard what was said. My nurses would never say that." Doubting that Connie would do anything about the incident, Celia made an appointment with Jeffrey Allen to report both the incident and her conversation with Connie. Celia hoped Jeffrey would share her indignation and take the matter up with Connie. However, he responded briskly, "Connie is in charge of the nurses, and I have every confidence in her and the way she handles her staff." Since then, two similar situations had occurred involving nurses who spoke disrespectfully to residents, and Celia's frustration grew. In her social work classes Celia had been studying about treating clients with dignity. *That's obviously not treating the client with dignity!* she observed.

When her internship began, Celia continued in the activity director position Mondays, Wednesdays, and Fridays while completing her social work internship on Tuesdays and Thursdays. Celia felt lucky when the ASU field director approved her internship at Country Acres so she could keep earning a salary while completing her degree. She thought, *I know I have to work out my separate roles at the agency, but I'm determined to make this work.*

"I am going to be the very best social worker I can be!" she told Mark Lewis, the ASU field director. "I want everyone to be proud of me."

"Celia, you have many assets that you bring to the internship," Mr. Lewis responded. "You're a mature student with a great deal of life experience. Also, you've worked with older adults for over 12 years, so I know you're comfortable working with them. Plus, you're already familiar with the community resources in Lynn County, and you know from experience how limited the resources are. That'll be helpful to the new social work director at the nursing home since she's not from a rural area."

"But I have something I am a bit worried about that I want to discuss with you," Celia volunteered. "The staff now sees me as the activity director. I wonder if they'll take me seriously as a social work intern. I hope they let me do the job because I know I can do it!"

"It's going to be a bit tricky," Mr. Lewis acknowledged. "You're going to have to be clear to yourself and to the staff about your roles—when you are the activity director and when you are the social work intern."

"I believe I can do that," Celia said.

"Before you leave, let me review the supervision arrangement with Sally Jones, okay?"

Celia nodded and Mr. Lewis continued, "Because Betty is new to the job and new to working in a nursing home, I've asked Sally Jones to function as a preceptor, and your administrator has agreed to continue to pay Sally for her time. You'll work mostly with Betty, but Sally will meet with you and Betty for supervision and consultation each week, and she'll oversee your internship. I think Sally's going to work with Betty to help her learn the job, too. I believe this will work out great for you, Celia."

"I'm excited about it!" she responded.

Leaving Mr. Lewis's office, Celia thought about their conversation. *So Mr. Lewis thinks my internship may be "tricky,"* she mused. *It does need to be clear about the "hat" I am wearing when I am at work. I wonder if that is going to be tough. . . . But, he's right. I do have a lot to offer the nursing home and the residents.*

MR. BROWN

Celia's first challenge about which "hat" she was wearing came two weeks after beginning the internship. One Monday in late August, while reviewing Mr. Brown's medical chart to prepare his activity assessment, she found it difficult to focus just on his level of social involvement and activity stimulation needs. *I would like to view him as a social worker would view him . . . I need to practice thinking like a social worker.* She decided to read his full chart, including his business file (which described his financial situation), his social history, and the initial psychosocial assessment that Betty had completed.

As Celia read, she learned that Bobby Brown, a 47-year-old Caucasian male, had arrived at Country Acres on June 2, 2001, after several weeks of hospitalization for injuries from a motor vehicle accident that included brain injury and trauma. His diagnosis included basilar skull fracture, subarachnoid hemorrhage (bleeding onto the surface of the brain, most often caused by a break in a blood vessel at the base of the brain; often occurs without warning and is life threatening), pneumothorax, and gastrostomy tube status. Bobby Brown relied on a gastronomy tube (G-tube) because he could not swallow as a result of his injuries. The G-tube, a feeding tube inserted into his stomach, provided all his nutrition. In addition, he was unable to use his arm and had difficulty walking. As a result, his ability to perform Activities of Daily Living (ADLs) was very limited.

Mr. Brown had a long-standing history of alcoholism, and there was no record of detoxification occurring at the hospital. According to the notes in the medical chart, he had not requested any alcohol while in the facility.

The chart reported other problems as well. Mr. Brown was homeless and living in his van at the time of the accident. The accident totaled his van, and, along with it, destroyed all his possessions. As a result, he had many psychosocial needs including a stable environment, clothing, personal care products (e.g., toothbrush, deodorant, shaving supplies), as well as amenities for his room, such as a television or radio for stimulation.

Betty and I were successful in getting him clothes and everyone else helped out, Celia recalled. *We got him a television and radio, and a few staff members brought personal care items for him. But I wonder about his financial resources?*

Celia reviewed the business file to learn more about Mr. Brown's situation. Betty's notes revealed that on June 2, the day Mr. Brown was admitted to the nursing home, the hospital discharge planner called Betty. She explained to Betty that she had urged Mr. and Mrs. Brown to apply for Medicaid to help pay for nursing home care, and Mrs. Brown had assured her that she would help Mr. Brown with the application.

Celia knew that any persons applying for Medicaid assistance for nursing home placement needed to qualify medically and financially. Medically, Mr. Brown required the type of care provided in a nursing home, thus meeting one criterion set forth by Medicaid to pay for his stay. Financially, his records showed that his earnings and assets were small enough that he could be classified as "indigent," and therefore he met a second criterion. Because he had no resources of his own to apply toward payment for his stay in the nursing home he was considered "full vendor," which meant that Medicaid would assume full financial responsibility for his nursing home care.

Celia read further in the notes. On June 5, 2001, three days after Mr. Brown's admission, Tina Gonzalez, the business manager had informed Betty that he was not eligible for Social Security Disability Insurance (SSDI) because he had a sporadic work history, and lacked the number of "quarters" or time to qualify for the program. *Hmmm,* Celia thought, *according to this file, Mr. Brown has no job, no SSDI, no savings, and no spending money. He needs Medicaid for sure.*

Celia continued reading to learn about the discharge plan. Betty had documented a conversation with Mr. Brown about the plans for discharge.

Celia read Betty's notes:

June 10, 2001—Met with Mr. B. to discuss plans for discharge. Wanted me to know he plans to go home with his wife, Julie Brown. Mr. B. stated, "I am not here cause I am old, I'm here for rehab; I'm not staying a day longer than I need to." SW will continue to follow-up with resident re: discharge plans.

Betty also had documented a concern about Mr. Brown's personal support system. He had no children, nor did he identify any significant friends in his life. Betty also had interviewed Mrs. Brown who reported that she and Mr. Brown were still technically married, but had separated prior to the accident. Betty recorded Mrs. Brown's words: "I felt sorry for him after the accident and came back just to help him but don't want to get too involved."

I found the same thing, Celia remembered, *when I completed my initial activity assessment back in June. He really has no support system.* Celia turned her attention back to the chart and continued reading, following Betty's documentation through the ensuing weeks.

It looks like Mrs. Brown keeps vacillating about her level of involvement, Celia observed. One week, Julie Brown had told Betty, "I plan for him to come live with me." Then, the next week, she would change her mind, and say, "Please don't call me anymore. I am not responsible for him."

That's so strange! What's going on? Celia wondered.

Celia's review of the chart confirmed that Mr. Brown had no financial resources and almost no support system. Mrs. Brown's involvement with him was sporadic. As Celia closed the chart and filed it away, she concluded, *There's a lot of work for Betty. I can help if she'll let me. I'm going to bring this up at our next supervision session.*

MEETING WITH MR. BROWN

On September 4th, just a few days after Celia had been looking at Mr. Brown's chart, Betty paged her to the social work office. "Celia, I just got an unexpected call from Julie Brown. She says she's been divorced from Mr. Brown since June, but didn't want anyone to know about it. She said she called him this morning and told him they were divorced. I know you have weekly activity visits with him, so I'm assuming you have a good relationship with him. Would you go visit him and see how he is doing about this news of the divorce?

"Sure," Celia responded, "I'd be happy to." *Finally,* she thought, *I get to do some real social work! I'm glad I reviewed his chart recently.*

Remember, you have your social work hat on now, Celia told herself as she approached Mr. Brown's room. She found him sitting in the dark seemingly staring into space. She knocked and called out, "Mr. Brown?"

"Yeah," he turned toward Celia and, in a subdued voice, said "come on in."

"Hi, Mr. Brown, I came to see how you are doing. I heard from Betty that Mrs. Brown called you this morning with some heavy news."

He sat quietly for a few moments looking at Celia. Then with tears in his eyes he responded, "I didn't know she had divorced me. She never told me before that she didn't want to be married to me anymore. She just told me today. I don't get it! Why?"

At first, Celia sat quietly and wondered what she should say. *He must really care for her. Why is she doing this to him?*

"Mr. Brown," Celia responded hesitantly, "this seems like a big surprise to you. I just want you to know we are here for you. How can I help you through this?"

He shrugged his shoulders.

Celia continued to sit with him for a half hour, listening to his confusion and grief, as he continued to ask why. Celia did her best to offer reassurance, "We're here to help you. I know it seems confusing now, but together we'll get through this."

NO MONEY, NO PLACE
TO GO. NOW WHAT?

The next day, Betty called Celia into the office and said, "Celia, I need some help with Mr. Brown. Tina has asked that we help him figure out his financial situation. Apparently the caseworker at DHS told her that Mr. Brown has missed all his appointments, and hasn't filed his Medicaid application. Tina thought Mrs. Brown was helping him with it, but now we find out that she wasn't."

"Oh," Celia said. "So what do we need to do?"

"Well, we aren't getting any money for him here at the agency, and Mr. Brown doesn't have any spending money.

"I was reading his chart the other day and wasn't sure what kind of financial and social support he had. I was going to ask you about him at supervision tomorrow when we meet with Sally," Celia said.

"Do you have a minute to look at his business record with me and see what's going on?" Betty asked. "I'd like to set a plan that you can follow and then get back to me with the outcome, okay?"

"I can do that," Celia said.

"OK. I have his business file here. Let's see what's in it."

As they reviewed the notes in Mr. Brown's record, Celia recalled, "You know, Mr. Brown told me that Mrs. Brown gives him a few bucks now and then. I don't know how much she gives him though. I've seen some of the staff giving him money and other things, like cigarettes and Dr Peppers, too. I think they just wanted to give him some extra help."

"Well, I can't stop the nursing staff from giving Mr. Brown money and cigarettes," Betty said. "It's not right, but it's their choice. If they want to do it, they will."

"That's true" Celia responded.

"I think the first place to start is with DHS," Betty continued. "We need to get him on Medicaid. His ex-wife isn't going to take him to that office, like she said she would back in July, so someone needs to go with him."

"Yeah, you're right about that," Celia agreed.

"OK, would you make an appointment for Mr. Brown at the Medicaid office, take him to the appointment, and, if need be, help him fill out the Medicaid application?" Betty asked.

"Sure, I can do that."

Celia made the appointment and two weeks later took Mr. Brown to the Medicaid office to meet with Janet Love, the Medicaid caseworker. Janet was very helpful and assisted Mr. Brown in completing the application.

Celia felt relieved, *I'm glad I didn't have to do that form! It's so long and complicated . . . it would have taken me forever to finish it with Mr. Brown. The caseworker really knows what she's doing.*

Within 30 days of the visit to DHS, Tina reported to Celia that Mr. Brown was receiving his personal needs check in the amount of $30 a month, and the nursing home was receiving payments from the State of Texas, and that he also received a check for $210 in past due monies.

TOO MANY CLIENTS, TOO LITTLE TIME

In October, during a weekly supervision meeting, Betty asked, "Celia, how has Mr. Brown been doing in activities? But more importantly, from a social worker's point of view, what have you been observing about him?"

"Well, he rarely attends any group activities," Celia responded. "He seems to be pretty much a loner, staying in his room most of the time lying in his bed. His ambulation has improved and he is able to get up and move around more easily and walk with limited assistance. I have seen him talking with staff, but he doesn't seem to engage much with the other residents."

"And even though he and Mrs. Brown are divorced, she still takes him out for home visits once in a while, at least, up until recently," Celia continued, "and sometimes for three days at a time. But she has stopped visiting and seems to want no contact with him. I don't know why she's stopped contact. Do you have any idea?"

"No," Betty said. "I looked to see if there was an explanation in the medical chart, and then I tried to call Mrs. Brown but she's not returned my phone calls."

"That's strange! But he really has been cooperative and behaving well in the facility. When I looked at the medical chart I saw that twice in the last two months he didn't receive his medications because he came back to the facility with 'alcohol on his breath.' But he was never out of line; he just went to his room and went to sleep."

"Celia, when I completed his social history and assessment in June, I said to myself, 'He's going to need a great deal of social work help to achieve his goal of returning home.' And, boy, was I right! You know, I have 129 residents that I'm responsible for. I'm so busy with other residents that it's too hard to find time to assist Mr. Brown."

Betty looked at Celia, who was fidgeting in her chair. After a moment, Betty said decisively, "There's not much more that can be done with Mr. Brown. . . . He doesn't have much going for him. This is hopeless! And other residents need my attention."

Celia held her tongue and reminded herself, *I'm just an intern. I don't want to make any waves, but, man, I can't believe she just said that! I thought we were here to help all the residents, not just those with resources. I just want to get out of this office before I say something unprofessional and get myself in trouble!* "Is that all for today?" Celia asked. Betty nodded and Celia quickly left Betty's office.

Over the next 20 days, as Celia continued her work as both the activity director and a social work intern, she became increasingly frustrated by the lack of activity on Betty's part to address and resolve Mr. Brown's numerous needs. She believed he needed and deserved more attention. One day, as she visited his room on her regular rounds, she noticed, *He's getting better. The G-tube is out, and he's up and walking with limited assistance. I want to help him in any way possible.*

As they were talking, Mr. Brown told Celia, "I really need to get my driver's license. I need some ID."

Celia thought for a moment, *He really does need a photo ID and maybe having the license would increase his self-esteem.* So Celia drove Mr. Brown to the Department of Motor Vehicles to get the ID, and she paid the $10 for it out of her own pocket.

Later that week, Betty asked Celia, "How did Mr. Brown get his license?"

"Oh, I gave him the money, and took him over there to get it."

"Why did you do that?"

"Why the twenty questions? What's the big deal?" Celia raised her voice, "It's $10! It made him feel better. Why can't I do that?"

Betty's voice was growing more tense. "Some staff members have voiced concern to me that you let him use his money to buy cigarettes. I know that you have used some of your own money to buy him cigarettes when he ran out."

"He has the right to smoke," Celia responded self-assuredly. "What he does with his own money is his business, not theirs. And if I buy him cigarettes, it's my money. Is that so wrong?"

I can't believe that she's picking on me, Celia thought. *All I'm doing is trying to help Mr. Brown! Ooh, if she wasn't my supervisor for this internship. . . .*

"Celia, it is a big deal," Betty concluded the conversation. "Maybe we need to talk with Sally, and see what she has to say."

"I WANT THE CASE . . ."

The next Thursday, during the weekly supervision time, Celia commented to Sally shortly after Betty left the room, "I don't think Betty is doing much to help Mr. Brown."

"What do you mean, Celia?" Sally asked.

Celia responded, "I really want to work on his case as a social work intern, not as the activity director. Mr. Brown needs a lot of help so he can be discharged, but Betty isn't doing anything about it. When I ask her about places he could move to, she just shakes her head and says she is working on it, but he doesn't have much money."

"OK, before we go any further, will you go get his chart for me?" Sally asked.

Sally reviewed Mr. Brown's chart, while Celia sat quietly. After she finished reading, Sally said, "Celia, I have to agree with you. From reading this chart, I think things are at a standstill. Let's talk with Betty. Maybe there is something going on that we don't know about."

When Betty returned to the office, Sally asked her, "What are we doing for Mr. Brown? Are we providing the services he needs?"

Betty responded carefully, "I tried to get what he needs but he needs so much and he doesn't have much going for him. Especially without much money, it's hard to get the services he needs. I have other residents to work with, and not a whole lot of time. I guess I just put him on the back burner."

"You're right, Betty, you do have other residents vying for your attention and services; and there's always too little time. You know, I reviewed his chart and discussed Mr. Brown with Celia. I think this case may be a great opportunity for Celia to practice her social work skills, including discharge planning. What do you think?"

Betty nodded, "If she has the time, let's see what she can do."

Celia added Mr. Brown to her social work caseload that afternoon. At that point, he had been residing in the facility for five months. That afternoon, to refresh her memory Celia again sat down again with Mr. Brown's chart. As she read it, she thought, *He's different from the other residents in the facility. He's younger and has a variety of needs and concerns—minimal financial support, no family support, no community support, and nowhere to go once he leaves here. But he's got great potential and really needs social work intervention. He's essentially starting over with nothing. I believe I can really help him.*

As she thought about her new case, Celia realized that one of her biggest frustrations was that she felt the staff was judging Mr. Brown unfairly for his previous lifestyle. Moreover, she remembered overhearing a staff member say, "He's a nonperson floating around taking up space." Just a few days earlier, a nurse had said within earshot of Celia, "He brought it on himself with his drinking."

It seems they don't even think he is worthy of attention, Celia concluded. *Oooh, this is so maddening! Can't they see he has a right to try and we're supposed to help him!* After reflecting a few moments she resolved, *I need to advocate for my client; the staff cannot dictate how he should live his life! I need to think about how to handle this.*

THE LAST STRAW

A couple of days later it happened again. While standing within earshot of the nurses' station, Celia overhead Mary Lou Frances, one of the station nurses, say, "I wish the social worker would get him out of here. He doesn't belong here."

Sarah Spelling, a charge nurse from another unit, asked, "Who are you talking about?" Apparently Mary Lou gestured because Celia did not hear a response. *I wonder who she is talking about.* As she looked around the corner she saw Mr. Brown sitting nearby looking at the two nurses. *They're talking about him.*

Sarah responded, "Oh, I know . . . he doesn't have much money, but he still manages to smoke. And, he's an alcoholic. He was probably drunk when he had that wreck. He'd be better off dead, than living like this."

Mary Lou added, "Yeah, he's always begging me for a cigarette. He's got it good now, free room and board. What a waste of taxpayers' dollars!"

As Celia walked up to the nurses' station, Sarah quickly turned and said, "Hello, Celia!" Turning back to Mary Lou, she said, "Well, Mary Lou, I need to get back . . . see you at break."

Celia said a perfunctory "Hello" as she passed Sarah but inside she was seething. *I cannot believe what I just heard! I am so sick of them talking ugly in front of residents like they aren't even there. . . . He could hear them! This happens again and again. I think it's abusive! I've got to do something, but what?*

Case 5

Carla Fights the System[1]

MARY ANNE POE

It was September 15, 2002, and a sunny Friday afternoon beckoned. Yet Carla Hudson, a social worker with the Women's Resource Center, had one more meeting before the weekend began. One of her clients, Maria Velasquez, was simply not getting the extra help she needed from Head Start, so Carla was on the way to meet Maria's new case manager, Andrea Nichols. Though trying to assume the best, she still wondered whether Andrea would respond any better than the previous worker. *If not,* Carla thought, *their refusal looks like ethnic discrimination!*

WOMEN'S RESOURCE CENTER (WRC)

WRC began in 1975 as a volunteer organization serving women in violent domestic situations. By 2002, WRC had expanded to nine offices offering services in twelve counties in north Alabama. Sonya Vickers had been the executive director for eight years. She supervised a staff of 20, all baccalaureate level

1. This decision case was prepared solely to provide material for class discussion and not to suggest either effective or ineffective handling of the situation depicted. While based on field research regarding an actual situation, names and certain facts may have been disguised to protect confidentiality. The author and editors wish to thank the anonymous case reporter for cooperation in making this account available for the benefit of social work students and instructors. Copyright © 2005 Thomson Learning.

workers except for two LCSWs recently hired to do sexual assault therapy. Funding for the agency came from a variety of state and federal grants, United Way, and private donations. Services were offered free of charge. In 2001, WRC responded to about 10,000 crisis calls and provided services for some 4,000 women and their children. The agency staffed a 24-hour crisis line, operated three shelters, provided individual and group counseling, offered hospital and court assistance, and managed a speaker's bureau for community education.

About half of the staff at WRC were Black or biracial, including the executive director. About 70 percent of those served by the agency were White and middle-aged and close to 30 percent of the clients were Black. Very few clients of other racial or ethnic backgrounds called the crisis line or sought services.

The region served by WRC was largely rural. Jasper, the largest town, had a population of 85,000. The overall population in the area was about 65 percent White and 35 percent Black. Only 1–2 percent was Latino or other ethnicities. Just like many regions of the country, though, this area had a growing Latino population, primarily Mexican migrant workers. Schools, clinics, government agencies, and businesses were struggling to adapt to the changes brought by these newcomers. Most of the local Latino population was poor with only limited ability to speak English. Their housing, employment, health, and education needs created challenges for the social institutions and agencies in an area that still struggled to manage sometimes volatile Black/White relationships.

CARLA'S BACKGROUND

Carla Hudson grew up in Jasper, Alabama. She had worked in various social service jobs before finishing her bachelor's degree in social work in May 1999. One of only two Black students in her cohort at a small private college, Carla was well acquainted with the experience of being a minority group member. Furthermore, she was a 30-year-old, nontraditional student in a very traditional setting. She had excelled in the BSW program, though, and graduated with honors. The social work program recognized her skills and her passion for social work by naming her the "Social Work Graduate of the Year." The job at WRC opened for her immediately after graduation.

Carla began her BSW career as a crisis counselor. In more than three years on the job, she had grown and developed professionally. Carla's primary role was to respond to crisis calls and follow up with case management. She listened to the women and their stories and made referrals to various services the agency offered.

After just a short time at the agency, Carla realized that women affected by domestic violence in the surrounding rural area needed a support group. So she started a group on Monday nights. The group had thrived. Carla was an advocate for women affected by violence and her clients easily sensed her commitment to them and to justice. She operated from a strengths perspective that empowered them to regain control of their own lives. Her co-workers saw Carla as a role model—a strong, assertive woman who had overcome her own difficulties with poverty, abuse, and discrimination. They recognized her passion for her work and for making the world a more just place to live.

MARIA VELASQUEZ

As a 24-year-old Mexican immigrant, Maria Velasquez was one of the newcomers that the community of Jasper was struggling to accept. She had two children, ages 6 and 3. Maria moved with her family from just outside Chihuahua, Mexico, to a Mexican immigrant community in Stafford, Virginia, when she was in seventh grade. She and her family became U.S. citizens about three years later. She learned enough English to graduate from the local high school, but still had great difficulty reading and writing it.

Maria had a long history of sexual abuse by her stepfather. One time her mother actually caught the stepfather fondling her. Maria told Carla that her mother just cried and cried, begging her, "Forgive him, forgive him, please." Perhaps these experiences made a relationship with Rodney Johnson, a 21-year-old Black man who was enlisted in the U. S. Army, attractive to her when she was 16 years old. He became her ticket out of an unpleasant home environment. They married when she was 18 years old.

Soon after they were married, the U.S. Army moved Rodney and Maria to Spain for about a year. By this time, Rodney's abuse of Maria had already begun. When she refused sex, he raped her. He used other forms of sexual abuse against her as well as ridicule and threats. She once reported an assault to military authorities while in Spain, but subsequently dropped charges because of his threats. When Rodney completed his service with the Army in 1997, they moved to Jasper, his hometown. Their first child, Lartyania, was just two months old at that point.

MARIA'S FIRST CALL TO WRC

Maria first called WRC three years later, in July 2000. She had just given birth to her second child, a son they named Raul. Maria was napping on the sofa in their living room with the newborn and Lartyania just behind her. Rodney woke her by pouring hot water on her face and shouting at her, "Get your lazy butt up!" He grabbed her arm and slung her toward the front door, leaving the two children on the sofa. Maria scrambled to the door and ran to a neighbor's house and called Debra, the wife of Rodney's brother. She came to Maria and after more arguing and fighting with Rodney in the front yard of their house, she helped Maria get the children and leave. Debra gave Maria the number for WRC and said, "Call these people, they will help you."

Carla was the worker who received the initial call from Maria. She listened to Maria's story and offered various options: Maria could press charges, take out an order of protection, and/or be assessed for admission to one of WRC's shelters. When Maria chose to enter the shelter, Debra brought Maria and the children to the WRC office for the assessment. Carla gave Maria a folder with the policies about the shelter and an application, and encouraged Maria to take her time with them. Carla was at her desk straightening a bit while she gave Maria time to read over the material. After a short time, she noted that Maria had stared for a long time at the papers and shuffled them around. She seemed downcast, almost embarrassed. *I wonder if she's able to read these papers?* Carla mused. With that thought, she got up from her desk and joined Maria at the table.

"I think I am finished with those things now. Let's review this together," Carla said.

Carla carefully read it all to her, being sure that Maria understood the importance of confidentiality and secrecy about the location of the shelter. Maria had no driver's license, transportation, or money. Though Carla had no difficulty understanding Maria's spoken English, it seemed clear that Maria's literacy skills were limited.

Carla learned more about Maria's dire condition as she continued to assess her situation during those first weeks Maria was in the shelter. She talked with Maria almost every day, either at the shelter or by phone, in order to understand Maria's background better. Rodney had prevented her attendance at English classes. He had closely guarded the family's financial business. He was unemployed, but had income from the military that she had known nothing about. He secured loans, used credit cards in Maria's name, and manipulated all their financial matters, making her vulnerable.

Over the next few weeks, Carla assisted Maria with applications for government-sponsored assistance programs. She was eligible for vouchers from Women, Infants and Children's program (WIC), $375 per month in food stamps, and $185 per month from Temporary Assistance for Needy Families (TANF). Maria was Carla's first Spanish-speaking client and Carla had not realized how difficult it could be for clients with little English literacy to negotiate the application process. All the paperwork was overwhelming. Though Carla usually did not go with clients to the Department of Human Resources (DHR) office, she did accompany Maria on occasion because Maria told her that the workers would not explain what she needed to do and she could not read the instructions well. Maria told Carla repeatedly, "The workers act rude to me."

Carla assisted Maria by helping her read applications and complete them. Carla helped her get a job at a hotel and enroll Lartyania and Raul in Head Start. Carla and the other women in the shelter comforted Maria during those long weekends when Rodney had the children for visits. When other women in the shelter helped her learn to drive, she got her driver's license by taking a Spanish language version of the test. Soon, Carla began encouraging Maria to go to school where she could gain reading and writing skills in English.

After living about six months in the shelter, Maria had become stronger. One day she said to Carla, "I think I am ready to go home."

"You do? What do you think will be different now?" Carla responded. *Oh, no! I hope she doesn't decide to go through with this,* Carla thought.

"I think I can manage it now. I feel strong. This place is nice, but it's not home."

"We have group tonight. Why don't you bring it up there and see what the group thinks," Carla suggested.

That night Maria did bring up her plans to return to Rodney. Others in the group were adamant, "Don't go, Maria," they said almost in unison. But this was a decision that only Maria could make. Carla supported Maria's right to choose for herself.

"Each person has to live with her own decisions and needs to use her own judgment," Carla reminded the group when Maria defended her choice to return to Rodney. "We may not think this is the best thing for Maria to do, but she has to decide for herself."

When she was preparing to leave a few days later, Carla encouraged Maria one last time, "Keep your checking account a secret and deposit part of each paycheck without letting Rodney know. And please keep coming to group."

"I will," Maria assured her with a hug.

THREE MONTHS LATER

"I've made a big mistake," Maria sobbed, when Carla answered her call to the crisis line early in April, just three months after Maria had moved out of the shelter. "It's all started up again."

Maria wanted to move back into the shelter. Carla worked on those details after getting assurance that Maria and the children were safe. Carla learned that Maria had kept the promise to keep her money hidden from Rodney and by now had saved a total of $1,500.

In the next few months, Carla counseled with Maria individually and continued to lead the support group that Maria attended. Maria was glad to be back in the shelter. She had changed jobs and was working at Wal-Mart. Carla connected Maria with another local relief agency that helped her secure an apartment and a car. This agency introduced her to a local church group that paid her rent and utilities until she became eligible for Section 8 housing. Maria moved into her own apartment in September, but continued in WRC's support group and stayed in regular contact with Carla. Maria had help from legal services getting a divorce, but she still had to contend with Rodney's having visitation privileges with the children.

Despite the couple's divorce, Rodney's abuse continued and Maria's fears increased. Several times, Rodney followed her car as she left work. Once she had moved into her own apartment, he sometimes called her 20–25 times a day. Another time, he slit her tires and cut the brake lines on her car. He even towed her car from the Wal-Mart parking lot to his house one day. Carla helped Maria get a recording device installed on the phone. With Carla's encouragement, Maria eventually had Rodney arrested for stalking. She got an order of protection. At one point Rodney contacted the Department of Children's Services and reported that Maria was abusing her children. He made visitation times with the children stressful.

In spite of Rodney's harassment, Maria continued to gain confidence and power in her own life. With encouragement from Carla and the women's group, Maria returned to school in January at Jasper Community College (JCC) with the help of a Pell Grant. She started out in remedial classes. She struggled to keep up with her young children, a job, and her school work. After the first semester, Maria found herself on academic probation because of poor grades in her English classes. How could she get some help with her studies? Her teachers had suggested that she get a tutor. They had offered no other help. She could not afford private tutoring.

Maria turned to Carla and the women's support group again for help. Her failure at school was a great discouragement. Carla realized that Maria needed more support in her educational pursuits.

"Have you discussed your problems at JCC with your Head Start caseworker?" Carla asked one night after group. "I think they can provide support for a parent's education."

"They've never offered any help," Maria answered. "I'll ask."

HEAD START

Maria's daughter, Lartyania, had been in Head Start for almost three years. Raul, Maria's son, had also been admitted to the Head Start program. Each family in Head Start was assigned a caseworker who provided an array of social services including referrals, family needs assessments, and crisis intervention. In particular, Head Start provided educational assistance to parents of children in their program when the parent's education or lack of education affected their children.

"My caseworker told me to talk to my teachers at JCC," Maria reported to Carla the next week at group. "I told them I had already asked and that I had even checked on tutoring offered by the school."

"I'll call the caseworker," Carla said. "Maybe I can get some help."

The next day, Carla called the caseworker, Kristin Wilson, to inquire about the situation.

"Tell Maria to ask her teachers at JCC for some extra help," Kristin suggested to Carla. "Maria has a good job at Wal-Mart and doesn't need any more help from us."

"But she has already discussed her problems with her instructors. She can't use the tutoring services there because of her job schedule. Maria can do a lot better helping her kids if she has good language skills. Surely you see this," Carla responded.

THE DILEMMA

For the next several months, Carla's work with Maria focused on trying to help Maria get the education and especially the English reading and writing skills she needed. Kristin seemed continually unresponsive to the difficulties that Maria experienced, even after several conversations with Carla. Maria's teachers at JCC had not extended any extra help either, according to Maria. When she asked them for help, they always referred her to the tutoring services on campus. Carla called JCC to explore what support services were available to students. They had a tutoring program but the tutoring services were not available when Maria could use them. Over time, Carla became convinced that Head Start could be helping with tutoring. She did not understand Head Start's resistance to providing this help.

Finally, Carla decided to advocate more aggressively at Head Start and contacted the Head Start director to present Maria's case. In this conversation, the director assured Carla, "I will investigate and ensure that Maria will get the services she needs and deserves."

A few days later, Maria called Carla and sounded very upset. "Head Start is mad at me. My worker, Miss Kristin, called me today. She fussed at me. She said, 'You got me in trouble with my boss. I told my boss that Head Start had helped you with your rent and utilities and lots of other things. We've got lots of people to help. We have given you lots of help!'"

"I told Miss Kristin," Maria continued, "'But you haven't helped me with rent and utilities. Why would you tell her that?' Then Miss Kristin said to me, 'That doesn't matter right now. Don't discuss Head Start business with Carla any more. We'll handle Head Start business'."

Carla responded that she would follow up on this for Maria. Curious whether Head Start had provided any help with rent, she asked Maria to bring in all her records about rent and utilities. Although Maria had not been able to read the monthly statements, she had carefully kept them together in a shoebox. When Carla reviewed the records she discovered that Kristin was wrong. According to Maria's records, Head Start had not provided any of this help to Maria. Carla wondered, *Why is Kristin lying? What is the problem over there?*

Carla decided to call Kristin again to plead for assistance with tutoring one last time but Kristin was not in charge of Maria's case any more. She had left Head Start just a few days before for another job. Carla learned that Maria's case had been transferred to Andrea Nichols, and made an appointment for a face-to-face visit the next day. *I'm going to get to the bottom of this,* Carla thought. *Maybe Andrea will be more helpful. I don't like getting in another agency's business, but I think this is discrimination. What other reason than discrimination could it be? Do all*

Spanish-speaking people in this town have so much difficulty getting services? Maria has had a hard time at almost all the agencies I have helped her with. Maybe I should contact that Latino legal advocacy group in Montgomery. I guess I'll see how this visit goes first, Carla's problem-solving thoughts rambled on.

Andrea greeted Carla at the appointed time. Once they got settled in Andrea's office, she asked, "Now, tell me again about the problem with Maria. I have known Maria for a while even though she was not on my caseload."

"I am still concerned that Maria is not getting all the services she should be getting. She needs tutoring for her studies at JCC," Carla said.

"Uh, uh, uh, Maria," Andrea mumbled, twirling her long, blonde hair around her fingers as she talked. "Maria can read English when she wants to. She is just not trying. I guess she throws away any messages we send home with her children." Carla was surprised by this response. *How does Andrea know this? She must have talked with Kristin. Those two blondes have decided together not to help Maria.*

"I don't think you understand the difficulty she has. I have worked with her for several years now. She speaks English fairly well. She just can't read it. She can't pass her courses because of it," Carla replied. "Are you going to help her or not? Head Start is supposed to offer these services to parents." Carla was beginning to feel the heat in the room. *They just think we're troublemakers.*

"I don't know what else we can do for someone like Maria. She's just not trying," Andrea said.

"Is there some reason that this Mexican immigrant can't get the services that Head Start is supposed to offer?" Carla asked. "She should have help that she needs with tutoring. Her English reading and writing directly affects her children's welfare. That's what the Head Start parent services are for, right?"

Carla already felt that she was at a dead end with this worker, too. *I wonder what the director thinks about this situation. How can I force the system to give Maria the help she needs and that they are supposed to offer?*

"She wouldn't follow up on it. She just wants you to do everything for her. They're all like that. She just needs to study more," Andrea summed up her thoughts to Carla.

"So, that's it? That's what you think about it? Well, I guess I will be in touch. I know she needs this support but it doesn't seem like there is any help here," Carla said while getting up to leave. She could hardly see straight she was so angry. *Andrea is a new worker for Maria and she hasn't even given her a chance. This is not the end of the story for me,* Carla thought. *I am tired of hassling with this discrimination. What else could it be?* She did not know what to do next, but she had to take it to the next level. *Should I call the director again? Should I call the Latino legal advocates in Montgomery? Or should I just give up on Head Start and look elsewhere for help for Maria to pay for the tutoring she needs?*

Case 6

This Could Get Messy[1]

SCOTT W. TAYLOR

After coming home from a long day at Interfaith Mission House in mid-November 2003, Angelina Pettit and her husband sat down for supper and discussed special plans for hosting singles from their congregation, Church at Union Station, for Christmas Day. They agreed that no one should be alone on Christmas, so they always invited people who lived alone or had no where to eat dinner.

"By the way," Philip said as they cleaned up the evening dishes, "I invited Jacob and Raymond Estes."

"I wish you had told me first that you wanted to do that." Angelina stopped drying dishes for a moment, "this could get messy, honey."

VOLUNTEERING AT INTERFAITH MISSION HOUSE AND CHURCH AT UNION STATION

Interfaith Mission House (IMH) was a small, 501(c)(3) faith-based organization located in downtown Dallas, Texas. As an interdenominational, holistic Christian ministry and social service agency, it addressed issues of poverty, unemployment,

1. This decision case was prepared solely to provide material for class discussion and not to suggest either effective or ineffective handling of the situation depicted. While based on field research regarding an actual situation, names and certain facts may have been disguised to protect confidentiality. The author and editors wish to thank the anonymous case reporter for cooperation in making this account available for the benefit of social work students and instructors. Copyright © 2005 Thomson Learning.

drug and alcohol abuse, homelessness, and other serious social issues and needs by providing adult ministry programs to those in the inner city. The programs included:

- A women's support group that met weekly and offered a safe environment for participants to discuss issues and concerns, develop leadership skills, and provide each other with spiritual and emotional support
- A computer lab and self-paced tutorials to help clients build resumes and computer skills, empowering them and opening up opportunities for professional development
- Employ, a job readiness program funded by the North Texas Workforce Development Board through TANF grants under Charitable Choice guidelines
- The Communion House, a residential substance abuse treatment program for men
- The Walking Bridge, a Christian-based living facility for men who had completed the residential treatment program and worked on establishing themselves safely back in society, eventually moving into Zion
- Zion, a small intentional community where unrelated individuals and families chose to live together in a household under agreed on Christian principles

Since its inception in 1984, IMH had gained a national reputation for its work in the Dallas area. Individuals and families from around the city, churches, and other nonprofit agencies volunteered their time to help with the adult ministries. The organization was also known for its close relationship with Church at Union Station, a nontraditional "blue jean and ball cap" congregation sponsored by and located a few miles from IMH. In 1990, the executive director of IMH, Thom "Buddy" Corgan, his wife, Joan, and Jeremy Schmidt, a college student from the University of North Texas, began a weekly Bible study at Union Station with homeless men who lived along the loading docks of the rail station. As weeks grew to months, more homeless men, Dallas residents, and college students joined the group, and relationships developed into deep friendships. Often attendees would sit on the pavement because there were not enough chairs, and some people would bring their own lawn chairs. Much of their time together was spent discussing issues related to homelessness, such as the need for clothing, food, and shelter, as well as social assistance and ways to break the cycle of poverty. Many alcohol and drug addicts chose to enter into the Communion House, while others took advantage of the computer lab and other social services offered by IMH. In 1992, Church at Union Station became a recognized congregation, and leaders developed by-laws, implemented a mission, and hired Buddy as their full-time pastor. In addition, all IMH staff attended Church at Union Station, contributing to an effective social service ministry. Within the community, people always mentioned IMH and Church at Union Station together; they would say the two organizations were like "two peas in a pod." The local newspaper often reported on the good work IMH and Church at Union Station were doing in collaboration with one another.

PHILIP AND ANGELINA PETTIT

Attracted by the positive press coverage and wishing to contribute, Philip Pettit began volunteering at Interfaith Mission House in 1996. As a computer programmer for 15 years, he enjoyed working in the computer lab, helping others enhance their skills. In 1998, he and Angelina began visiting Church at Union Station on Sundays, wanting to find a place of worship as well as a place to volunteer in the community. Quickly joining, and becoming leaders a couple months later, Philip agreed to be a Sunday school teacher and a leader of a men's fellowship group, consisting primarily of recovering alcohol and drug addicts who gathered weekly to discuss various joys and struggles in their lives. Meanwhile, Angelina volunteered to lead a women's Bible study, and a couple months later they moved into the Zion community wanting to share and live out their Christian values with others. After interacting with homeless persons and addicts once again, Angelina had begun to wonder, *Could I use my social work skills when working with this population?*

Angelina, 47 years old and a licensed social worker, had gained much of her professional social work experience at Child Protective Services (CPS) in Dallas. She began work at CPS after completing a BSW at the University of North Texas in 1979. She spent 15 years on staff and had practiced with a variety of clients representing many ethnicities, as well as with colleagues from diverse backgrounds. As an investigative social worker, Angelina developed strong skills working with troubled families, often with abusive parents who did not meet their children's basic survival needs. During this time she learned a lot about the challenges of "living in poverty" and realized that working with the disenfranchised and the oppressed was what she did best.

But toward the end of her tenure, Angelina started to realize that she was so busy making a difference for the state's kids at CPS that her three children— Austin, Jacelyn, and Sophia—were beginning to fall "through the tubes." She was ready for a change and decided to pursue her professionalism in another venue. Unsure about what she wanted to do, when her children entered junior high school she took a three-year hiatus from social work, and stayed at home to take care of them full time. Not entirely satisfied with being a "stay-at-home" mother, Angelina realized that working with people in need provided much meaning for her. On a Wednesday in 1999, after a Bible study at church, she shared with Philip, "It's time. I really feel the need to look for a job in social work again, one where I could work with and care for people who are struggling to make it in the world."

Knowing that she was looking for a job, Buddy Corgan asked one day after church, "Angelina, I would like for you to be Director of Social Services at IMH and use your good social work skills from CPS." A few weeks later, Angelina gratefully accepted the opportunity. For the next four years, her job duties included supervising a walk-in center, overseeing the Communion House, the Walking Bridge, and Zion, and managing the cases of all clients within each social service program. Other responsibilities included crisis intervention, information referral, counseling, and supervising volunteers and social work interns. Angelina deeply enjoyed her work at the faith-based agency. As she told Philip, "I really love working at IMH; my clients and I feel free to discuss our faith, if the client wants to." She found herself remembering childhood experiences volunteering with community ministries sponsored by Second New Life Church (SNLC) of Dallas.

A WOMAN OF FAITH

Angelina's strength in practicing with families in poverty was fueled by the Christian values she embraced as a child while going to church with her parents. Attending almost every Sunday at SNLC of Dallas, Angelina began at an early age to learn about the inner-city poor who were living simply and suffering daily. SNLC was located in the heart of downtown where many homeless people, including families, and people addicted to alcohol and illegal drugs resided on street corners every night. With a desire to meet the basic needs of this disenfranchised group, the congregation developed a small community ministry geared to provide them with basic necessities. These needs typically were clothes, food, and shelter. Many homeless persons and addicts began attending services regularly and some even joined the church as members. During holidays, families in the church, including Angelina's, would often invite them to their home for dinner and a chance to experience family. Angelina's family was particularly known to invite singles to their home when others in the church would not.

Angelina also believed that living in the community where she worked not only helped her identify with and better understand the poor, but was also consistent with her values. She often told people, "To live with those who suffer and have great need is how I try to develop community intentionally." Philip occasionally loaned his tools and other building supplies to neighbors, including Angelina's clients, and helped them in remodeling their homes or fixing their vehicles. Angelina and Philip lived around her clients many hours a day. They believed that their work at IMH and leadership at Church at Union Station went hand in hand, and caring for people, including Angelina's clients, was important to living out their faith.

ANGELINA'S CLIENTS

As Director of Social Services, Angelina was the only social worker at IMH and responsible for ensuring all new clients received the appropriate services. Some clients only desired short-term services in order to build resumes, learn computer and job readiness skills, or to participate in the spiritual and emotional support groups for women. For them, Angelina developed a specific short-term treatment plan to meet their needs. Most of her clients, however, were at IMH for a long-term stay at the Communion House. Angelina worked with these clients to develop long-term treatment plans to help them graduate into the Walking Bridge, and hopefully later into Zion, the intentional Christian community. Zion's mission was to provide a place for individuals and families to live out their Christian values while supporting each other through community building. Many clients heard of IMH and its social service programs while attending the Church at Union Station; this was the case for brothers Jacob and Raymond Estes, two of Angelina's clients who were members at the church and later decided to enter into the Communion House for rehabilitation.

Jacob Estes had been working with Angelina and living in Zion for approximately a year when he tested positive for drug use on his monthly urinalysis. Up until that point he had begun to take a leadership role at the church, meeting with other struggling homeless men once a week for coffee and prayer. "Jacob, you were doing so well," Angelina had told him sadly. "But you broke the rules, and we have to release you from Zion. I really hate doing this, and if you come back you can reenter the Communion House." Despite moving out of Zion, Jacob continued in Philip's fellowship group at church, and two months later he began receiving services again from IMH.

Jacob's brother Raymond had graduated from the Communion House and showed personal and professional growth while living in the Walking Bridge. He moved into Zion, and took a job at IMH as a mentor for drug and alcohol addicts. Because he lived in the Zion household, Angelina was his social worker. She was also Raymond's supervisor at work. "You have learned how to deal with your addiction well," Angelina commented to Raymond before offering him a job, "and you have done a good job of letting me be your social worker at IMH and your fellow congregant while at church. It's been challenging, yet you pay attention to boundaries, including being my neighbor." Angelina was proud of Raymond and what he had accomplished. She was also glad that Raymond was in Philip's fellowship group at church, and was learning how his faith gave him a reason to strive for a good life and to help others who were struggling.

A BALANCING ACT

As a member of the National Association of Social Workers, Angelina was very familiar with its Code of Ethics, which warned social workers not to get involved in dual relationships with clients. She had first learned about the code as a BSW student 24 years before and prided herself in her commitment to practice ethically. Because all of Angelina's clients at IMH attended the Church at Union Station, she made it a part of her routine in the contracting phase to explain carefully to her clients how her role was different at church than when they saw her as social worker at IMH, and vice versa. Sometimes, on Sundays, her clients caught her at church, and wanted to discuss their needs and concerns at IMH. She had a standard response: "While I am at IMH, I am a social worker; while I am at the Church at Union Station, I am a member and Sunday school teacher. Therefore, unless it's an emergency, it would be best to discuss your needs while we are at IMH."

Another example of how Angelina managed dual relationships occurred when Philip's Bible study group decided to go to Six Flags Over Texas. The men wanted to bring their spouses, especially because most of the spouses attended the women's Bible study at the same church. After Philip asked Angelina if she would like to go, she responded, "I really need some time off, and this seems like it would be fun. Plus, I could hang out with my girlfriends while you ride the roller coasters." Because it was a church function, Philip drove the church van. Only after everyone piled in, Angelina realized that she was sitting next to some of her clients from the addiction recovery group. As they rode in the van, some of them started embellishing their drug stories, Angelina quickly stated, "Hey guys, no war stories!" They understood this language because "war stories" were what they shared during their group meetings. *I needed to say that to remind them that I was their social worker,* she thought. Once they returned from an exhausting, but fun day at the amusement park, Angelina waved good-bye and shouted, "Thanks for letting me go with you even though I am not in the men's or women's Bible study." Angelina left, believing she handled these dual relationships ethically and professionally, but it was not always that easy.

Since Angelina started working with her clients, she felt like she was doing a good job of managing her work, church, and neighborhood relationships. Most men who lived in the Communion House, the Walking Bridge, and Zion, and who attended Church at Union Station, understood that Angelina was everyone's social worker. Raymond and Jacob knew that Philip, their Sunday school teacher and fellowship leader, was her husband. Furthermore, having the church directory and being neighbors, they had access to their telephone number and had stopped by their house occasionally for short visits with Philip. But sometimes she wondered, *Could my being embroiled in so many dual relationships eventually cause problems?*

ANGELINA'S DILEMMA

After dinner one November evening, Angela got up from the table and began clearing the dishes. "By the way," Philip said, "I invited Jacob and Raymond Estes."

"I wish you had told me first that you wanted to do that." Angelina stopped drying dishes for a moment. "This could get messy, honey."

"I forgot you worked with them, but I still don't think it is a big deal," Philip said as he left to watch TV. Angelina continued putting away the dishes in silence, thinking about her situation. Realizing Philip had already invited

Jacob and Raymond over for the Christmas dinner for singles, she considered thoughtfully, *What will their coming over and eating a meal that I have cooked do to my role with them as their social worker? Will this damage my therapeutic role with the guys? Or will it help for Jacob and Raymond to see me without my "social work hat" on?* Angelina felt caught between her desire to care for people as part of the congregation and her commitment to avoid troublesome dual relationships. *How do I deal with these situations when I live and worship with my clients?*

Would this be any different? She wondered. *This time, they would be coming over to visit with both of us for a holiday dinner. What would other social workers think? Will Philip understand my dilemma?* Angelina had so many questions: *Will having my clients in our home socially compromise my professional ethics or what I believe; or is it possible to keep both? So far, I have been able to set boundaries with my clients, telling them, "This I do in the church context; this I do in a social work context; this I do as a neighbor." But, now I am really tired of dealing with these messy situations, and I am beginning to second-guess my actions. Is it alright for my husband to work as a volunteer with the same people who are my clients? Will he think I am being ridiculous if I tell him I am uncomfortable with having them in our home? Am I really managing these dual relationships ethically?*

Case 7

In Need of Support[1]

SHARON B. TEMPLEMAN
DEBBIE GOVE

As Linda drove to work on a crisp October day in 1999, she was frustrated. She couldn't help but wonder, *Why does everything have to be so hard in this town? If this were happening in Fayetteville it wouldn't even be an issue! Here in Casper, I may have to make up stories and disguises just to get my clients the services they need.* Linda felt herself getting anxious. In a few hours she would begin a telephone conversation with six men that would determine her next course of action.

CASPER, NORTH CAROLINA

Situated where North Carolina's Piedmont region meets the Coastal Plain region, the town of Casper was located two hours from the coast between two river basins, the Neuse and the Cape Fear. When it was first settled in the 19th century, inhabitants thrived on agriculture, particularly tobacco and cotton; the rich soil and mild climate also allowed production of soybeans, corn, hogs,

---

1. This decision case was prepared solely to provide material for class discussion and not to suggest either effective or ineffective handling of the situation depicted. While based on field research regarding an actual situation, names and certain facts may have been disguised to protect confidentiality. The author and editors wish to thank the anonymous case reporter for cooperation in making this account available for the benefit of social work students and instructors. Copyright © 2005 Thomson Learning.

cattle, and poultry. Since the 1950s two textile factories and several businesses and restaurants provided additional opportunities for employment.

The 1990 U.S. Census reported that the population of Casper was 10,000. Fifty-six percent were White, 34 percent Black, 9 percent Hispanic, and 1 percent were classified as "Other." The median household income was $26,534. Other small rural communities, also thriving on agriculture and industry, surrounded Casper. Fayetteville was the nearest city; it was about 45 minutes away and had a population of 125,000.

Casper loved to celebrate its heritage and traditions. The town was founded in the 1890s when the railroad from Fayetteville came through the area. Many of the buildings downtown had fallen into disrepair in the mid-20th century but, since the 1980s, had been restored when the area was registered as a historic district. Each fall the citizens gathered for Harvest Days, begun in 1950 to honor the importance of agriculture in the region. There was also a Dogwood festival in the spring, which featured food, rides, and the crowning of the Dogwood Queen.

Newcomers, particularly those from cities, described Casper as "conservative" and noted that the town seemed "stuck in the 1950s." Located in the southern Bible Belt, Casper took religion very seriously. The many churches in town were full on Sundays. Like in other small towns in the South, the majority of the worshippers were Christian, primarily Baptist, Presbyterian, and Methodist. There were seven Baptist churches, two Methodist, one Presbyterian, and one Catholic church on the main square—all the houses of worship were Christian. There were no synagogues, mosques, or temples. The small minority of people who did not identify themselves as Christians either did not participate in weekly services or they drove to Fayetteville weekly to join others of their faith.

Religious traditions influenced the values that were expressed in the town's ordinances. Stores were closed on Sundays, with the exception of a few stores that opened after 1 PM. Wine and spirits were never sold in grocery stores, nor on Sundays. The town was "semi-dry," meaning that restaurants had a limited license to sell alcoholic beverages, which required consumers to purchase a membership to order alcohol.

DAYBREAK IN CASPER

Daybreak was a small privately funded nonprofit center that offered outreach, testing, prevention, medical treatment, counseling, information and referral, and case management to people with HIV/AIDS. It was founded in 1987 by Rodney Wyers, a gay man who grew tired of watching friends die of AIDS, mostly alone and without support. His friends were unable to keep doctor's appointments due to lack of transportation and often did not have their basic needs met, such as food and utilities. Rodney did not have a formal education or experience in social services but simply started where he could. He began having garage sales to raise money. He also began asking for help from the community of Casper. More often than not, he was rebuffed.

Especially in its early years, an agency like Daybreak serving people with HIV/AIDS had great difficulty developing financial resources locally because of stigma and fear resulting from a lack of knowledge and understanding about the disease. Appealing to their "Biblically based value system" many citizens of Casper viewed HIV/AIDS as "due punishment" for the "sin" of homosexuality. This value system discouraged community members from contributing monetary or in-kind support for Daybreak and basically created an unspoken "zero tolerance" policy for homosexuality. Many community members lacked the knowledge and understanding needed to support people infected with the disease.

IN NEED OF SUPPORT

Although raising support locally was difficult, Rodney had more success with federal sources. With help from friends, Rodney wrote a grant proposal and received federal funding in the amount of $6,000. He turned his house and garage into a warehouse and began stockpiling food and other supplies. Rodney recruited everyone he could to deliver food and provide transportation to doctor's appointments. He continued to take baby steps toward his dream of having an agency to serve persons with HIV/AIDS and he was making progress. By 1990, Rodney had obtained enough funds to rent a small office space and to hire the first case manager. The agency was licensed as a nonprofit, 501(c)3 agency and officially named Daybreak. There was still little support from the community of Casper. The community ignored the agency, pretending that it didn't exist.

By 1994, Rodney was struggling with burnout and wanted to leave Daybreak. He had successfully applied for numerous grants and had built Daybreak to the point that he could turn over operations to the executive director, Anita James. James had a PhD in Education and experience as an administrator in the Casper school system. When she came to Daybreak in 1994, she supervised three case managers who were experienced in various social service arenas, but none had any formal education beyond high school. She also provided oversight of an outreach worker/educator, a driver for the agency van and a receptionist/volunteer coordinator.

LINDA SUMMERFIELD

Linda Summerfield grew up in Casper and had been surrounded by its conservative values. She grew up admiring her grandmother, a "natural helper" in Casper. People turned to Maddy Bagby for advice and a helping hand. Maddy cared for ill citizens of Casper when professional services were unavailable or unaffordable. She provided personal care from bathing to feeding as well as helping with domestic duties like laundry and house cleaning. Wanting to help others as her grandmother had done, Linda decided to pursue a degree in social work. She commuted to Fayetteville State College, about 45 minutes away, and earned a BSW degree.

After graduating in 1995, Linda married her high school sweetheart, Ron Summerfield, and took her first job in Casper as a new social worker at Humanity General Hospital. Linda was the social worker for the hospital's rehabilitation unit, a position normally filled by an MSW. The State of North Carolina required that rehabilitation units hire either a full-time social worker with an MSW or a BSW social worker who was advised by an MSW consultant. Dr. Garcia, Linda's social work professor, had highly recommended Linda for the job and agreed to serve as the MSW consultant so that Linda could have the job. Linda was thrilled. *This will be a great challenge for me,* she thought, *and I know Dr. Garcia will be there to help me along.*

Working in the rehabilitation unit proved to be both a challenge and a continued learning experience for Linda. She provided an array of BSW interventions, but her favorite was group work. Under Dr. Garcia's supervision, she began group sessions to help patients cope with the life-changing events that accompanied their need for physical rehabilitation. The group work proved to be very beneficial for patients who were losing their independence due to leg amputations, strokes, and other physical challenges. Linda soon realized that there was a need for a community "stroke support group" so she did some research, contacted some previous patients, and began a task group to organize and start up the stroke support group. The group was a big success and as the clients became empowered, Linda was able to take a backseat in the group. Although Linda attended the groups to offer support, the group members actually planned the agenda, provided their own snacks, and found guest speakers. Linda was excited that she had been able to get the ball rolling and then turn the game over to the players. *So, this is what empowerment is really about,* she thought.

In September 1998, Humanity Hospital bought out the rehab center, and Linda and other rehab center employees were not allowed to continue working in the unit. They were given 30-days notice to find new jobs. Meanwhile, Linda and Ron had become parents of two children and she desperately needed to help support the family. Having the required qualifications, she applied for the job at Daybreak and was offered a job as case manager.

LINDA GOES TO DAYBREAK

Linda was the first social worker hired at Daybreak. Her title was Client Services Director, which meant she met weekly with the other case managers to provide support and direction as well as carrying her own caseload. She also helped Dr. James, the executive director, with administering policies and following state regulations, writing grant proposals, and raising funds.

At the outset, Linda had limited knowledge about HIV/AIDS, its means of transmission, or the populations in which the disease manifested. During the first week at work, she struggled with constant fear of contracting HIV. *What if I bring this disease home to my husband or children? What if I catch it and die— who will raise my kids?* However, as she learned more about the population, her fears quickly turned to genuine empathy and concern for the clients of Daybreak. Within two weeks she knew that she was in the right place; she loved her job.

LEARNING ABOUT HIV/AIDS

Through research Linda came to understand the myths and truths about the diseases of HIV and AIDS. Until coming to Daybreak, Linda had only distant relationships with those who had the disease. She began doing research on the Internet and found useful information from the National Institute of Allergy and Infectious Diseases that stated:

> Acquired Immunodeficiency Syndrome (AIDS) was first reported in the United States in 1981 and has since become a major worldwide epidemic. More than 830,000 cases of AIDS have been reported in the United States since 1981 and as many as 950,000 Americans may be infected with HIV, one-quarter of whom are unaware of their infection. Many people infected with HIV have no symptoms. Therefore, there is no way of knowing with certainty whether a sexual partner is infected unless he or she has repeatedly tested negative for the virus and has not engaged in any risky behavior.

Linda learned that AIDS was caused by the Human Immunodeficiency Virus (HIV) in which cells of the body's immune system were killed or damaged in such a way that the body's ability to fight infections and certain cancers was destroyed. What astounded her most were the effects of this disease on the health, relationships, and lives of those infected. And, the large number of cases of HIV/AIDS in this rural region of North Carolina startled her. *Before I started working at Daybreak, I thought HIV/AIDS was an urban disease.*

During the first six months, Linda worked with six male clients, all of whom had HIV or AIDS.

She kept notes on each one:

> **Frank:** Early 40s, Caucasian; never married, lives in Casper, restaurant manager in Ward, works long hours. Needs personal space. No one knows he's gay, may get fired if his boss finds out about HIV/AIDS. Five dogs, no social life or support system. In prison for 2 yrs. (1989–91); selling marijuana (but client reports never using drugs himself). Support system includes mostly drug users, Frank is disconnected from them. Says he wants to, in some way, mentor or adopt a young boy, as this is what brings the most joy to his life. Does realize that his prison record will prevent

this. Frank's health is "like a roller coaster." As of September 1999 health is good, but until Spring 1999, had been very ill for 6 months. Afraid to come to Daybreak for services. On October 19, 1999, I went to the restaurant, pretended to be business acquaintance; delivered medications and provided supportive counseling.

Kevin: 38 years old; Caucasian; lives with his mother in Ripley [a half-hour drive from Casper]. Single, works at his uncle's electrical business as a bookkeeper; father not in the picture; mother elderly; Kevin is her caretaker. Mother knows he is gay and that he is HIV positive. Caring for mother and his health are biggest concerns. One brother, but the two are not close. Strikes me as personable, jovial, fun to be around; laughs and jokes a great deal; usually gives me big hugs. Describes himself as "a touchy/feely person." Kevin does not have AIDS. Very few know he is HIV positive. Takes good care of himself, follows his recommended medical regimen. Before diagnosis, had many friends, partied often, says he was "the life of the party." After HIV diagnosis, Kevin started isolating himself. Very concerned about passing HIV on to others; completely eliminates all intimacy. Does not believe there is such a thing as safe sex.

Jeff: 34 yrs. old; Caucasian, lives in Baywood [a very rural community 45 minutes from Casper], works at hardware store; secretly gay. Extended family lives in Baywood and he grew up there; knows everyone. Sees people that he knows often, but "feels no connections with any of them." Until illness, went to Fayetteville often to be with circle of friends who were his support network. Was secretive about his friends in the city and as he got sicker, quit going to see them. Even though I have been seeing Jeff since December 1998, he still is lukewarm toward me; provides info only when I ask, responds in a "businesslike" style. If conversation is too personal, he retreats. Health is deteriorating; does not take good care of himself; copes by using denial, acts as if "this isn't really happening." Symptoms: enlarged lymph nodes or "swollen glands," lack of energy, weight loss, frequent fevers and sweats, frequent yeast infections, persistent skin rashes or flaky skin and short-term memory loss.

Tim: Age 25, Caucasian, has AIDS; small frame, a bit "delicate" looking; cute, easygoing, frequently looks scared. Worries about his image and what people will say about him. Has lived in Henderson [a town about 30 minutes from Casper] all of his life. Said in session, "I wish I weren't gay; if I could change this I would because it has caused nothing but problems." Socially, stays in touch with a few high school friends; goes out to eat with them less and less, very fatigued. Numerous side effects from medications, including diarrhea, that keep him at home. Frequently acquires opportunistic infections, which are caused by viruses or bacteria [that usually do not make healthy people sick]. Had a job in a gift shop, but owner questioned frequent use of sick leave; eventually quit work; fought to get disability benefits, which was difficult to explain to his family. He told family members he has cancer. NOTE: Tim insists that I never call his home!

There were two clients who were less involved with Daybreak than the other four. Linda provided some case management for them, but knew less about them. When they came in, they spoke of medical appointments, medications, and other services, but rarely discussed personal issues. Both received services before Linda came to the agency, so she never conducted an initial assessment, which would have revealed more personal information.

Jason: mid-30s; Caucasian, gave up support system when he moved from Fayetteville to Madison [a mid-sized rural town approximately one and one-half hours from Daybreak]. Works in a food market; fairly healthy, very private; and asks little of me.

Darrell: Early 30s, Caucasian, fairly healthy; lives in Casper, rarely comes to Daybreak. Account manager with NCE, the electric company. When he seeks services, he is focused, detached. Does not have AIDS.

Linda could see the impact that this devastating disease had on each man. Their social lives had nearly halted due to health factors, fear, and the stigma they endured in public. Each of them talked to Linda, but they needed more. *I give empathy and support,* Linda sighed to herself, *but I'm not what they need. I haven't walked in their shoes. No matter how hard I try, I can't really understand.*

Linda tried to find ways to help her clients get support. Once each month Daybreak held activities to bring patients together for socialization and support, but some of her clients were so afraid of being "found out" that they avoided these agency activities. They were far too private and reluctant, fearing the devastating consequences of being "discovered" as persons living with HIV/AIDS. Linda understood. *I don't want them to be discovered and then harmed in some way.* She remembered a recent situation where, as a result of rape, a young mother in Casper contracted HIV. The school rejected her son and their church shunned both of them. To protect herself and her son, the woman moved away from the area.

Still, their isolation is not good, thought Linda. *I wish I could bring them all together for support, like my clients at the rehab center.* Her clients' situations reminded her of a saying of Benjamin Franklin: "A man wrapped up in himself makes a very small bundle." She also remembered the old cliché, about safety in numbers. *My clients need each other!*

EXPLORING ALTERNATIVES

Linda began wondering whether group work might be beneficial for these six men. This was her first experience in direct practice with people with HIV and AIDS, but her experience at the rehab center had shown her the power of support groups. *I have seen clients in groups really help themselves and one another.*

Convinced that group support might be beneficial for her more isolated clients, Linda began tossing around the idea of starting a support group when she was meeting individually with her clients. Some expressed interest. But geographical distance, jobs, isolation, and fear of being "found out" prevented them from participating.

Disappointed and frustrated, Linda began to seek alternatives to traditional support groups. Her research led her to numerous articles on various spiritual groups and groups that appeared "cult-like" and even to some interesting participant–run groups. One that she found in a social work journal caught her attention. It was about telephone support groups in rural areas where transportation, distance, isolation, costs, and other factors made it difficult for members to meet. *This seems perfect! I wonder if we could try that here at Daybreak. It would be exciting to see whether we could make it work.* She began calling the six clients to present her latest idea.

CHARTING NEW TERRITORY

After a month, the men agreed to meet one time via telephone meeting and to only talk about the medical aspects of HIV/AIDS. Charting new territory for the agency, Linda brought Frank, Kevin, Jeff, Tim, Jason, and Darrell together via telephone. All six of these men had declined to meet face to face. As Tim told her, "It's too risky . . . my family doesn't even know that I am gay or that I have HIV; I'm sure not going to reveal this to total strangers." Likewise, Jason said, "No way! I have enough hassles with this disease as it is . . . I'm not about to announce to the world that I have HIV . . . if anyone found out I would lose my job." After much encouragement by Linda, the six men consented to "meet" one time by conference call. All decided to remain anonymous by using aliases and sharing no personal information.

The first meeting was 30 minutes late in getting started due to complications with the telephones. After making most of the arrangements, Linda found that the office did not have an adequate conference call system, which was frustrating but not surprising in an agency with limited resources. She arranged for all of the men to call in to the office at noon, when other employees were at lunch. With their permission, she then put all phones on speaker, all reaching into a hallway, and the men communicated by phone in this manner.

At first, members began getting adjusted to the group. They introduced themselves only by first names or pseudonyms. They had agreed ahead of time that they would not share where they lived or worked. By the end of this meeting everyone was laughing. The laughter relaxed everyone. They laughed at the situation and, imagining Linda in the hallway with all the phones, they even laughed at Linda. Members seemed to feel comfortable talking about their medications. By the end of the first meeting, they all agreed to "meet" again in the same way and at the same time the following week and to continue on a time-limited basis (six weeks) so that no one felt pressured.

MOVING FORWARD

In the second meeting, the members picked up where they had left off the previous week, discussing medications, side effects, and expenses. As in the first meeting, the second and third meetings focused primarily on the disease.

By the fourth meeting, members were discussing personal issues such as isolation. "I'm disappointed that I won't be able to adopt a child," lamented Frank. "I regret getting involved in selling drugs."

Tim longed to be back at work. "I get so bored," he said. "My mind needs to work even if my body won't cooperate."

By the end of the session Linda realized the tone was different. *They're connecting! This is exactly what I was hoping for. In fact, this is going even better than I imagined.*

Halfway through the fifth meeting, one member asked if they could exchange names and phone numbers, which was a departure from the original agreement. Linda was caught off guard by the question. *I don't know quite how to deal with this,* she thought. *I surely don't want anyone to feel pressured to reveal this information!* She cautioned them regarding the exchange of names and phone numbers but finally, after much discussion, she left the room so she could not hear them on speakerphone. That way the decision rested solely with the members and with the agreement that anyone who wished to hang up could do so. For 10 minutes those who stayed on the line could discuss anything they wished to talk about. As she exited, Linda said to herself, *Yes, this is working!* When she returned, the men told her that that four of the six members had shared names and telephone numbers.

During the second half of the fifth session, Linda encouraged them to take the next step by forming a face-to-face support group with her as facilitator. "You have so much in common," she told them. "First, you all have HIV, AIDS, or both. You all struggle with similar life-changing side effects of the disease and the side effects of the medications. Support groups address feelings of isolation, depression or anxiety . . . just the kinds of issues you have expressed in the telephone group. And it helps people make changes so they feel better and improve the quality of their lives."

"Yeah," Jason retorted, "but we still live in this conservative, redneck, rural area where prejudice runs rampant, I've heard enough hate-crime stories . . . I don't want to be a part of one."

"I intentionally stay away from family and friends," Darrell insisted. "I even moved recently because my neighbors made gay-bashing comments. I am not interested in being found out."

These two were especially against meeting face to face. With one week remaining in the six-week contract, the others expressed interest in transitioning to a face-to-face support group format. Although Jason and Darrell did not want to meet face to face, they agreed to continue with the telephone group if this became an option. As the meeting ended, they all agreed to give more thought over the coming week to continuing the group in some fashion and to discuss the issue further at the last meeting.

Just after the fifth meeting ended, Dr. James returned from lunch and stopped to speak with Linda. "I know that there is only one more phone meeting left and I am glad," Anita started. "I know you think the telephone thing is working, but it is just too difficult to clear the office for the time that you need to set up and 'meet.'"

Linda sat listening, not knowing yet how to respond as Anita continued, "Others need access to their offices and we need to be open over the lunch break so that clients can stop by when they are free."

"Anita, the men are not sure they want to meet face to face, especially two of them," Linda explained. "And even if they wanted to, where could we meet? You know they can't come to Daybreak without people suspecting they have the disease. What about purchasing a conference calling system that the men can call into? I have worked so hard to help them connect! I need some more time to try and make this transition."

Anita was already shaking her head as Linda was speaking. "I'm sorry, but we just don't have the funds. And without the technology for group conference calls here at Daybreak and with no funding allocated to this project, you need to either terminate the group or find another way to handle it."

DECISION DAY

Before the last meeting of the six-week telephone support group, Linda sat down to gather her thoughts for the meeting and jot some notes about her goals for the meeting. She had gently broached the topic of face-to-face meetings last week. Today, she would need to either persuade the group to meet face to face or talk with them about termination. *Even though they face similar problems, each one has his own unique needs,* she thought. She reviewed her notes from the first meeting.

All were Caucasian gay men; only Kevin and Darrell were openly gay. All had HIV and had been seen individually since first coming to Daybreak. Within the Casper area, they lived 50–60 miles apart in small towns. Although most worked, all were very private; none had revealed his HIV status to anyone other than health care professionals. None had a partner or family support. All were embarrassed to take medications in public because there were so many that they had to be stored in a large bag.

A common issue for all of them, thought Linda, *is that they have had no one to talk to or to discuss the disease with except me, until they met by telephone. This telephone contact has been so important!*

Linda was getting nervous. *Am I ready to facilitate this discussion again? It could get really emotionally charged. Are the guys ready to have this discussion?*

Linda worried that some members might still want to meet face to face and others might not.

Will the guys who don't want to continue feel pressured to keep going? Or maybe they would feel left out or abandoned if the rest of the group continued without them.

If the men did want to meet, the logistics could get complicated, and Linda knew she would be responsible for arranging everything. Because the men lived in different towns, everyone may not have access to transportation to a central location. Linda's thoughts turned to the details: *If the men do agree to meet, how will I get access to a meeting place in this closed-minded community? Nobody in Casper will ever agree to allow men with HIV/AIDS to use their facility for meetings if I am honest about the HIV/AIDS diagnosis. Maybe we need a cover story to disguise the purpose of the meetings. Is that ethical?*

She pondered that question for a while, wondering about the legal or ethical implications if the group decided not to be honest that they were an HIV/AIDS support group.

I want them to be able to meet if they want to, but finding a meeting place will be so complicated. On days like this, I really wish we lived in the city where this would not be such an issue!

Case 8

The Discharge Dilemma[1]

MACKENZI A. HUYSER
LAURA E. ZUMDAHL

"Diana, this is Kristen, from second floor."

"What's up?" Hospital social worker Diana Howard recognized her nursing colleague immediately.

"I'm calling about Mr. Mitchell," Kristen Voss continued. "The doctor signed off on him an hour ago, but we can't release him from the hospital until you meet with him and chart the plans for his discharge. We need you to come do this right away. It's busy in the ER this afternoon, and we need the bed."

Diana hung up the phone slowly. In her mind, Diana ran through the options she and Mr. Mitchell's sister had discussed, but she didn't feel at all confident about what they could provide to Mr. Mitchell. *What's the point of setting up services again? He's been in and out of the hospital three times this year (2000), and hasn't used the services we've arranged.* Diana felt stuck. *Should I bother to set up services even though I know he won't use them?*

1. This decision case was prepared solely to provide material for class discussion and not to suggest either effective or ineffective handling of the situation depicted. While based on field research regarding an actual situation, names and certain facts may have been disguised to protect confidentiality. The author and editors wish to thank the anonymous case reporter for cooperation in making this account available for the benefit of social work students and instructors. Copyright © 2005 Thomson Learning.

HOLLAND COMMUNITY HOSPITAL

Holland Community Hospital (HCH) was a 213-bed community-centered private hospital serving the residents of Holland, a small city in Western Michigan. According to the hospital's mission statement, HCH had "a commitment to continually improve the health of the communities we serve in the spirit of hope, compassion, respect, and dignity." This mission guided the hospital's efforts to provide access and high quality service to residents in the surrounding area. HCH was known for its community health outreach programs, including educational programs focused on nutrition, obesity, and cardiac heart failure.

HCH'S DEPARTMENT OF SOCIAL WORK

As one of many patient services, HCH employed social workers to support the efforts of medical staff. The Department of Social Work was responsible for handling internal referrals from hospital physicians and nurses as well as external referrals from Child Protective Services and police departments. For example, medical personnel called on social work staff to help family members cope with a patient's medical crisis and Child Protective Services caseworkers occasionally asked for help investigating possible child abuse of hospital patients. In addition to handling these crisis situations and referrals, the department was responsible for patient discharge planning. For many patients, this meant social workers assisted them and their families in arranging services after their discharge such as follow-up medical appointments or home health care services.

The Department of Social Work included four social workers: Carol Putnam, MSW, Sarah Wilson, MSW, Anne Peterson, MSW, and Diana Howard, BSW. They were an ethnically diverse team that worked well together and with the other hospital staff. Even though physicians, nurses, and social work staff worked well together, medical staff sometimes perceived the needs of individual patients quite differently than the social workers. Nevertheless, the social work staff worked to always present themselves as professionals while interacting with other hospital personnel. Because of this, the social workers took a united front on many of their cases. They had developed open communication with one another in an effort to ward off any conflicting perspectives and to better advocate for their clients.

Carol Putnam, with 10 years of experience in the medical setting, served as the director of the Department of Social Work. She knew well the stress of social work practice in the hospital setting. The fast-paced work, limited client contact, and documentation requirements made the job difficult and at times unrewarding. For these reasons, she encouraged the social workers to find a healthy balance in their lives and to not let the stress of their fast-paced jobs get out of control. She regularly led the department staff in discussions of how to relieve stressful situations. For example, she encouraged the staff to take a break for lunch each day, even when they were very busy and tempted to work through the lunch hour. Small things like this helped the staff to relieve stress and stay focused on their work.

DIANA HOWARD, BSW

Diana Howard returned to college in 1992 as a 36-year-old BSW student. Returning to school had been a challenge for Diana and her husband. It required balancing a busy school schedule and her husband's job with caring for her children and their home. Despite these challenges, Diana persevered because of her strong commitment to obtaining a bachelor's degree and her passion for social work. During her final semester, Diana worked as an intern in the mental health department of a local hospital. There, she learned how to gather intake information and had the opportunity to work with persons dealing with mental health issues such as depression. As an African American woman, she especially noticed how her African American clients experienced limited access to many mental health and general health care services. She believed that as a social worker she had a responsibility to advocate for her clients, and thought she could make a difference in how many of her African American clients could access medical services. Because of this sense of commitment and responsibility, she searched for a full-time position in the medical field.

After graduating in 1996, Diana took a job at HCH as a social worker. She knew from her internship experience in a hospital setting that medical social work was fast-paced, often stressful work. Social workers often had only a few days or hours to assess a patient's needs and make appropriate plans, and that could be difficult and stressful. Despite these issues, Diana liked the fast-paced environment and opportunity to work with diverse clients. She took the job as a hospital social worker aware of the challenges, but excited about the work.

One evening during her first year on the job, Diana was working in the emergency room when African American parents brought their 10-month-old boy for third-degree burns on his legs and buttocks. Diana met with the parents, a young couple, both only 19 years old. Through the course of her interview she learned that they had placed Peter in scalding hot water as a form of punishment for misbehaving. The couple spent the many weeks the child was in the hospital recovering by his bedside caring for him. The couple's behavior revealed that they loved their son, but they were inexperienced parents and did not know how to handle his behavior appropriately. Diana was thankful for a supportive supervisor who had helped her work through the challenges in this case and decide to report the couple's actions to Child Protective Services. Diana had learned from this experience that she often had to make difficult decisions that people may be unhappy about, however, all actions must be in the best interest of the client.

Diana had a very personal approach to her clients. Her quiet demeanor was indicative of her patient and loving attitude toward all those with whom she worked. She embraced the hospital's mission to assist all patients with compassion and respect. Diana took seriously her commitment to the NASW Code of Ethics and especially valued each patient's dignity and worth and right to self-determination.

JOSHUA MITCHELL
AND HIS MEDICAL HISTORY

Mr. Mitchell was a 75-year-old, African American man. Divorced from his wife many years before, he lived alone in a small home in Holland. His chart noted that he had been repeatedly admitted to HCH for medical problems related to diabetes and a stroke. At each discharge, the doctor had referred Mr. Mitchell to a social worker for assistance in discharge planning. Repeatedly, the social worker had made arrangements for home health care services such as a daily visiting nurse to administer his medication and homemaker services to clean his home and prepare meals.

Despite these plans to provide in-home services for Mr. Mitchell, the services were never fulfilled. Mr. Mitchell would apparently accept the services while he was a patient in the hospital so he would be released, but then refuse the services once he returned home. For example, after the last discharge, the home health nurse called Diana when Mr. Mitchell repeatedly refused to let the nurse into his home. Mr. Mitchell was fiercely independent and reluctant to have others help him. Although he was unable to care for himself and his condition would inevitably deteriorate after each discharge from the hospital, he was considered competent to make decisions regarding his care.

Medical records showed that home health workers called Adult Protective Services multiple times when they found him in deplorable conditions at home. Mr. Mitchell was incontinent and unable to keep himself or his home clean and thus home health workers often found him unbathed and dirty, lying in soiled linens. In addition, the home had developed a problem with mice. A worker from Adult Protective Services had come to his home to do an assessment and had been forced to call an ambulance on many occasions after seeing the decline in Mr. Mitchell's medical conditions, his unsanitary living conditions, and his refusal of services. The file indicated repeated admissions to the hospital over the course of three years.

TUESDAY MORNING, APRIL 6, 2000

Diana arrived at work early and was on the floor by 7:30 AM. After reviewing Mr. Mitchell's chart, Diana decided to tackle his case first. He had been re-admitted on Sunday morning, two days before. She looked on the assignment board at the nurses' desk to identify Mr. Mitchell's primary physician. After seeing that the doctor was not on the floor, she decided to begin by interview-ing Mr. Mitchell. She knew she wouldn't have much time with Mr. Mitchell because he was scheduled for discharge in a day or two. Diana found his room and knocked softly on the door as she entered.

Mr. Mitchell was sitting up in his bed watching television as commercials blared in his room.

"Good morning, Mr. Mitchell." Diana pulled the privacy curtain separat-ing Mr. Mitchell and his roommate. "I'm Diana Howard, a social worker here at the hospital. I worked with you a few months ago. Do you remember me?"

Mr. Mitchell gave a small nod in response.

"Mr. Mitchell, would it be okay if we turned off the television to talk?" Diana asked.

Mr. Mitchell grunted and shut off the television.

"I received a referral today to speak with you about services after you leave the hospital. From Dr. Marks's referral, it sounds like you will be discharged in a few days, and I want to speak with you about what services you may need when you leave."

"I don't need any services," he barked. "I can take care of myself."

"It appears from your chart that you have some pretty complicated med-ical conditions because of your diabetes," Diana continued.

"I don't need any services," Mr. Mitchell repeated. "Do you mind leaving now?"

Diana waited for a minute before she turned and walked out of the room. She tried to stay positive and think of another approach to talking with Mr. Mitchell.

As Diana left the room, she saw Sarah and Anne, her co-workers, talking with each other in the hall. Diana decided to consult with them about what her next step in Mr. Mitchell's case should be.

"How's Mr. Mitchell today?" Anne asked as Diana approached them.

"His chart says that he is nearly ready to be discharged, but he's still refus-ing to accept any of the services I can set up for him," Diana replied. "He's adamant he doesn't need help, but without assistance he keeps ending up back in the hospital."

"Maybe we're approaching this from the wrong direction," Sarah sug-gested. "We keep trying to arrange services for him, but that involves people he doesn't know or trust coming into his home. Maybe if he has a family member or friend who could assist him, he wouldn't be so reluctant to have help."

"That's a good idea," Diana said. "I'll see if I can find out what type of sup-port system he has. Maybe he has a family member who could help."

"We have to meet with a doctor now," Anne said, "but let us know if you need help, Diana."

"Thanks for the ideas, I'll let you know how it goes," Diana replied, as she turned to head back to the office.

TUESDAY AFTERNOON

Diana reached for the ringing phone, hoping it was the doctor returning her call. She had paged him several times in the past four hours and was anxiously waiting to discuss Mr. Mitchell's case with him before she proceeded.

"Hello, this is Diana," she answered.

"This is Dr. Marks, I'm returning a page."

"Yes, Dr. Marks, this is Diana Howard from the Department of Social Work. I called you to discuss Mr. Mitchell's case. I saw in his chart he's to be discharged in a few days and I'm trying to arrange services for him once he's at home," Diana said.

"He needs a visiting nurse to help with insulin for his diabetes," the doctor responded. "And judging from what I've read in his chart from the home health workers about his living conditions, he needs homemaker services as well."

"Those are the services I'd like to set up for him," Diana said. "However, the past several times he's been discharged from HCH we've arranged those services for him, but he's not allowed the home health workers to do their job. Because he's competent to make decisions for himself, I can't force him to receive services."

"I'm aware he does not like the services, however, it's your job to make sure he receives these services," Dr. Marks replied. "If he doesn't get help, he's going to have to go to a long-term care facility. I can't keep readmitting him to the hospital."

Diana thanked the doctor for his time and hung up the phone. But she felt confused about what to do next. She couldn't continue to set up services for Mr. Mitchell if he was not going to use them. But she also knew the doctor would not discharge Mr. Mitchell without having a plan to keep him healthy and safe. She remembered discussing difficult clients in her practice courses as a student, but she didn't realize how frustrating they could be. Diana felt stressed knowing she had only a short time to find the best plan for Mr. Mitchell. Perplexed, Diana decided to speak honestly about the situation with Mr. Mitchell when she met with him the next morning. She had thought more about what Anne and Sarah had said and she knew she needed to know more about Mr. Mitchell's support system in order to help him recover.

WEDNESDAY MORNING

"Good morning, Mr. Mitchell, how are you feeling today?" Diana asked as she entered the room.

"Fine," he replied.

"That's good," Diana said. "I wanted to discuss with you some medical plans for when you leave the hospital."

"I don't need any help at home," Mr. Mitchell stated, "I can take care of myself."

"I'm sure it's difficult to have help when you're so used to being independent," Diana replied, taking a different approach to the situation. "Because of your complex medical needs, however, the doctor thinks it's best to have some assistance for you once you're home so you can avoid having to be re-admitted to the hospital every few months."

"You can do whatever you want," Mr. Mitchell stated irritably, "but I'm not going to have anyone come into my home and help me."

"I know you don't like the home health workers coming to your home. You've done a really good job taking care of yourself in the past. With your medical condition, though, it seems like this might be a good time to evaluate your situation and make some changes. We can look at the options and find a solution that you're comfortable with. Do you have any family in the area that may be able to assist you?" Diana asked.

"I have a sister in Indiana, but she lives too far away," he replied.

"Do you have any neighbors or friends nearby that you see?" Diana probed.

"Not really. Just some lady from church," Mr. Mitchell said.

"Do you think she might be able to help you while you're recovering at home? Maybe she would be willing to help bring you groceries and check on you?" Diana asked.

"I doubt it. I'm sure she's pretty busy," he replied.

"Well, I see in your chart you have a signed consent form for your sister to be notified about your condition. Could I call and speak with her?" Diana asked.

"If you want," Mr. Mitchell shrugged.

"Okay," Diana said as she prepared to leave, "could we agree to talk with your sister and look at the options available to make a decision about your situation?"

Mr. Mitchell gave her a slight nod.

"I will let you know what your sister says when I call her," Diana told him as she left.

Diana promptly called Mr. Mitchell's sister, Mae Williams, and was able to speak with her that morning. When Diana explained her concern for Mr. Mitchell's situation, Ms. Williams insisted she would make the three-hour trip from Indiana to the hospital in hopes she could convince her brother to use the assistance available to him.

THURSDAY AFTERNOON

It was almost three o'clock when the nurse on Mr. Mitchell's floor called Diana to tell her Ms. Williams had arrived. As Diana hurried up the back staircase, she tried to mentally prepare what she would say to convey the seriousness of the situation to Ms. Williams.

As Diana entered his room she saw a woman who appeared a few years younger than Mr. Mitchell sitting by his bedside speaking to him.

"Hello," Diana said, "I'm Diana Howard, a hospital social worker. I spoke with you on the phone yesterday."

"Hello," the woman responded, "I'm Mae Williams."

"I'm glad I could speak with you yesterday. I appreciate you coming," Diana began. "As I said on the phone, I'm trying to arrange home health care services for your brother upon his discharge tomorrow . . . ."

"I don't need any help!" Mr. Mitchell interrupted.

Ms. Williams turned to look at her brother, "You need to let others help you or you are going to continue to end up sick and in the hospital. Will you please let Diana arrange some help for you?"

"No one is going to come into my home to help me. You can't force me to let people in. You can arrange services if you want, if that's what it takes to get me out of here, but I won't use them," Mr. Mitchell said, challenging the two women.

Ms. Williams stood and looked at Diana, "Can I speak with you in the hall?"

As Diana and Ms. Williams left the room, they could hear Mr. Mitchell grumbling under his breath, "People should mind their own business."

"Diana," Ms. Williams asked, "is there anyway I can overrule his decision and force him to use these home health care services?"

"Unfortunately, no," Diana replied. "The psychologist interviewed your brother and found that your brother is competent to make his own decisions and although we may not agree with him, he still remains in control. If he were not mentally competent, we would need your help in making decisions for him. Are there family members who might be able to care for him in his own home, since he's so insistent on staying there?"

"I can't care for him because of work and the distance, and we don't have any other family. I know he's supposed to leave the hospital tomorrow morning, but you can't let him go home like this," Ms. Williams pleaded. "He'll only become ill again and I'm afraid one of these times he won't recover."

"I understand you can't provide care for him," Diana said, "and private services such as home health care and homemaker services have not worked. The other options may be community services such as Meals on Wheels and other senior support services, but we'll probably run into the same problem because he probably won't let those people into his home either. A long-term care facility such as a nursing home might be another option, but those are expensive and may have a long waiting list."

"Let me try to convince him to accept some kind of help. It seems like he really wants to stay at home," Ms. Williams said.

"That sounds like a good plan. I'll connect with you before the end of the day," Diana said as she got up to leave.

LATER THAT AFTERNOON

Diana went back to Mr. Mitchell's room later that afternoon. Mr. Mitchell was sleeping, but Ms. Williams motioned for Diana to step out of the room to talk with her.

"I haven't been able to change his mind about accepting help," Ms. Williams said, "I feel like my hands are tied; there is nothing else I can think of to do."

Diana sighed disappointedly. "I need to check with my supervisor about what we can do; I will be in touch with you as soon as I know anything."

Diana walked down the hall hoping her supervisor would be able to assist her with the difficult situation.

"Hi, Diana, what's on your mind?" Carol asked as Diana walked into her office.

"I'm concerned about Mr. Mitchell," Diana began. "He's scheduled to be discharged today and I'm working on his discharge plan, but I'm worried he will refuse the services we arrange for him just like he's done in the past."

"Have you spoken with any family members who could be of assistance?" Carol inquired.

"I spoke with his only sister, Ms. Williams, who was also unable to convince him," Diana said. "He's mentally competent and we can't force him to receive the assistance. He doesn't have any family members able to care for him, either. The best option is home health services. However, if he doesn't accept some help he will never fully recover."

"Have you spoken to any of the other social workers?" Carol asked. "They may be able to help brainstorm ideas since they have worked with Mr. Mitchell in the past."

As Diana began to respond, her pager went off. Diana glanced down and recognized the phone number for the nurses' station on the second floor.

"I better take this," Diana said, knowing she had several clients on the floor who might need immediate assistance. Excusing herself, Diana quickly went to her office to return the page.

"This is Diana, I am returning a page," she said to the person on the other line.

"Diana, this is Kristen, from second floor," she said. "I'm calling about Mr. Mitchell. The doctor signed off on him an hour ago, but we can't release him from the hospital until you meet with him and chart your plans for his discharge. We need you to come do this right away. It's busy in the ER this afternoon, and we need the bed."

Diana hung up the phone slowly. She felt stuck. *Should I bother to set up the services even though I know he won't use them?*

Case 9

The Ridge[1]

LINDA MORALES
T. LAINE SCALES

"These kids have no one looking out for them up there at the Ridge and I can't do a thing about it!" As she threw her keys on the kitchen table, Tamara Simms made no effort to hide her discouragement.

In response, Johnny Simms stood up to give his wife a warm hug and tried to empathize, "Sounds like your home visit up at the Ridge didn't go very well."

"Bottom line," Tamara responded, "I don't have enough evidence to report something my gut tells me is very real."

The two sat silently for a few moments as tears began to roll down Tamara's cheeks.

"I know you had a tough day, but you gotta let it go, hon. Jaci and I need you tonight," Johnny said quietly, "you can look after us."

THE RIDGE

The Ridge was a poverty pocket in Sabrina County, located about eight miles north of Timberland, a rural East Texas town of about 28,000. In the 1950s, developers envisioned the Ridge as a self-contained community for white-collar executives,

1. This decision case was prepared solely to provide material for class discussion and not to suggest either effective or ineffective handling of the situation depicted. While based on field research regarding an actual situation, names and certain facts may have been disguised to protect confidentiality. The author and editors wish to thank the anonymous case reporter for cooperation in making this account available for the benefit of social work students and instructors. Copyright © 2005 Thomson Learning.

a "bedroom community" for Timberland. It was located in lush woodland, some of which was owned by the local paper mill and backed up to the Muddy River. When the developers realized that the land was in a flood plain, however, they abandoned the project and the land became virtually unmarketable. Gradually, white underclass families, many on fixed incomes, some working at minimum wage jobs, and some unemployed, moved in to the Ridge.

Approaching the Ridge, one passed through a "green curtain" of thick loblolly pines (though some of the stands had recently been clear-cut). A sharp curve in the road marked the entrance to this pocket of poverty. The main road into the community was black-top, but other winding roads into the community were dirt or gravel. The latter were passable except during heavy rains or flooding of the Muddy River.

Most residents of nearby Timberland avoided the Ridge. "Everybody knows there's drugs up there," they said. African Americans and Latinos from Timberland particularly avoided visiting the Ridge because they heard it was an extremely bigoted community, and could be dangerous for nonwhites.

Police officers and occasionally a few CPS workers from Sabrina County entered the community to investigate crime reports. Domestic violence was widespread, though the workers learned from talking to residents that many cases went unreported because few residents had telephones. These professionals observed that the housing conditions were "deplorable" and the streets were "filthy." They often described the whole community as "apathetic and hopeless."

Some people from Timberland referred to citizens of the Ridge as "white trash." They often joked about "an incredible accumulation of junk" in the yards: abandoned cars (a few yards contained more than 10 wrecked vehicles), toys, rusty appliances, half-burned heaps of trash, and broken furniture pieces. Several Confederate flags waved in the breeze throughout the community.

Despite the poverty and violence, CPS workers, law enforcement officers, clergy, and other helping professionals also recognized that the Ridge had strengths. Neighbors helped neighbors; they watched each other's children and shared food, rides to the grocery store, laundry facilities, and at times their homes. Extension cords were strung between mobile homes, as people shared electricity. The community included several social organizations: a Methodist church, a Baptist church, a fire department, and a fishing camp provided social opportunities for families. Young children from the Ridge attended school at average rates. Even when some of the roads were impassable on rainy, muddy days, they walked several blocks to meet the school bus that took them to Timbers Elementary School. However, teenagers attended at much lower rates. According to the records of the Timberland Independent School District, a high percentage of the teenagers who dropped out of high school were from the Ridge; many of them took low-paying jobs at age 16 or 17.

SCHOOL SOCIAL WORK IN TIMBERLAND
INDEPENDENT SCHOOL DISTRICT

Timbers Elementary School was housed in an 80-year old school building that was targeted for demolition as soon as the school district could pass a bond issue to replace several old school buildings.

Tamara Simms, BSW, worked for the Timberland Independent School District and was frequently called to intervene in situations that arose at the junior high school or three elementary schools. With more than 8,500 students, Timberland Independent School District employed three BSW-level social workers. Carla Harvey worked only with pregnant teens, while Jenny O'Conner was assigned to a special education unit. Tamara Simms "floated" between all the schools as the troubleshooter who dealt with health problems, truancy, poverty, substance abuse, and behavioral problems. She was frequently called to intervene in situations that arose at the junior high school or three elementary schools. But her primary assignment was to Timbers Elementary School. About 40 percent of Tamara's caseload of children lived within the Ridge community, and the rest were from Timberland.

Because social workers were relatively new to the Timberland school system, they had the additional challenge of proving their value to the system. Often they were perceived as "truant officers," "friendly visitors," or child protection workers. The social workers spent a lot of energy defining their roles for the school system, their clients, and their supervisor. The curriculum director, Mark Alinsky, supervised all three social workers. Mr. Alinsky was a highly experienced school administrator, but Tamara soon realized that he knew very little about social work.

TAMARA SIMMS

Thirty-two-year-old Tamara Simms had been married for 11 years to Johnny Simms. Johnny was a native of Timberland, his father having been a senior vice president at the local paper mill for many years. Tamara grew up in Dallas, but when they moved to Timberland, she made a good adjustment to living in rural East Texas. Tamara and Johnny were Caucasians living among a population that was about 60 percent Caucasian, 25 percent African American, and about 15 percent Latino. They bought acreage adjacent to her in-laws' ranch. Johnny graduated with a forestry degree in 1996, one year before Tamara graduated from East Texas State. He worked as an independent timber contractor. They had one daughter, Jaci, born in 2001.

Johnny always teased Tamara about being "a neatness freak" because she liked to keep an immaculate house, liked to keep order in her day, and never missed an appointment with her hairdresser. Still, she thought she had learned to make allowances for others who were not so compulsive as she. Tamara was happy doing school social work and planned to remain in that practice arena through Jaci's years of schooling.

Tamara had been engaged in school social work for six years, ever since she received her BSW in 1997 from East Texas State University. She was employed right after graduation by Timberland Independent School District as their first social worker. Tamara worked with countless families in those six years and had a reputation among the teachers and administrators in the school district for being very competent in her work.

ENCOUNTERING THE ANDERSONS

On September 8, 2002, Tamara ran into Ms. Collins, the fourth grade teacher, in the hallway just as the lunch bell rang. "Did you have any luck finding the shoes?" asked Ms. Collins.

"Great luck," said Tamara with a satisfied smile. "My friend who works at Noley's department store got a pair of Nike's donated. They're in my office."

"Good; can I bring Bobby Joe up to see you in a few minutes, after lunch?"

"OK, I'll look for you in a few minutes," Tamara replied.

The Anderson family was not new to the Timberland school system and not new to Tamara. Tamara recalled that Mr. Anderson parented alone because, as he said, his wife had "gone off somewheres." Tamara was especially familiar with him because he had a long-running conflict with Timberland Independent School District. He refused to get immunizations for his children. When a law had passed in Texas stating certain immunizations were no longer legally required, he had been the first to access that document and bring it to the principal's office saying, "See, I was right all along."

Ms. Collins had referred nine-year-old Bobby Joe Anderson because of his shoes. Ms. Collins had caught Tamara in the hallway the day before and told her that the odor of Bobby Joe's shoes was "unbelievably foul," and asked Tamara if she could help. Tamara knew from her experience with Bobby Joe that he also had other problems with personal hygiene, such as bad breath, and a general odor as if he had not bathed. This was not uncommon for families from the Ridge; frequently Tamara encountered families whose water had been shut off due to lack of payment or who actually never had running water in their homes.

When Tamara arrived back to her office, she found Ms. Collins and Bobby Joe waiting. "Hi, Bobby Joe. I've got a surprise for you!" said Tamara. Bobby Joe's face lit up in anticipation. Tamara noticed he was barefoot.

"I see Ms. Collins has already asked you to take off your shoes; that might give you a little hint about my surprise."

Meanwhile, Ms. Collins had tied up the old shoes and put them in a bag. "I'm taking these straight to the Dumpster," she whispered to Tamara. "I'll be right back," she announced to Bobby Joe as she passed by Tamara and went out the door. A few minutes later, when Tamara proudly presented Bobby Joe with the new shoes, she was taken aback by his response.

"I have to ask Daddy! Daddy will get real mad! I can't have new shoes, please give me my old shoes back. Please, please," he whined.

"OK, OK," Tamara tried to reassure Bobby Joe. "I will get your old ones. You wait here with Ms. Collins. It's all going to be OK."

Tamara went out to the Dumpster and retrieved the old shoes, using her Bengal spray to ward off the wasps that had built their home in the Dumpster, removing an abandoned toilet that someone had dumped there. A few minutes later, Bobby Joe seemed happy to have his old shoes back.

After Bobby Joe left, Tamara was determined to talk to Bobby Joe's "Daddy" and find out whether her hypothesis that there was no running water might be true. She also wanted to ask his permission to send home the new shoes.

Many Ridge families did not have phones, but the file indicated that the Anderson's had a phone number so she dialed it.

"Hello, is this Mr. Anderson?

"Yep."

"My name is Tamara Simms, school social worker at Timbers. I am calling about Bobby Joe's shoes."

"His shoes? What about 'em?"

"Well, we offered him a new pair today, but wanted to check with you if it is OK. His old ones had quite an odor."

"So?" he said in a cold tone.

"We wanted him to have a pair of good tennies so that the other kids would not tease him, but he seemed hesitant to accept these without your permission. But we can't allow him to attend school with shoes that smell."

"Well, I do the best I can! Do you know how much new Adidas cost these days, even at Target? More than I could afford on my income." Mr. Anderson's tone had become defensive.

"That's why we had hoped to help out, without of course offending you in any way," Tamara said gently. "We know you are doing the best you possibly can to care for your children."

Hmmm, do I know that for sure? Tamara thought. *But what else could I say? I do need to find out about their water situation though.*

"Mr. Anderson, do you have any problems with hot and cold running water?" asked Tamara.

"Of course we have water, lady. You must really see us as trash! I just couldn't afford $50 for shoes for Bobby Joe, that's all . . . If it's really any of your business."

"I know you are employed . . . what is it, er . . . Internet sales of some kind it says here in the file, but we all run into tough times financially."

"I'll just bet *you* run into tough times, lady."

"Can you tell me more about your Internet sales?" Tamara probed.

"Why do you need to know that anyhow?"

"Mr. Anderson, I'm just trying to figure out how we can best help you with your children."

"Thanks but no thanks. I'm hanging up now," he barked.

And with that, Tamara heard a dial tone.

LICE AT THE ANDERSON'S

About six months later, in April 2003, the school nurse, Ms. Cooper, referred eight-year-old Sarah Jane, a third grader who had severe blisters on her lips and was infected with lice. Ms. Cooper sent medicated shampoo and Vaseline home with notes, but as Ms. Cooper told Tamara, "Sarah's head is literally crawling with lice, and it doesn't seem that Mr. Anderson has used the treatment. Also her lips are raw and blistered." Apparently Mr. Anderson was not following the suggestions that Ms. Cooper sent him. This prompted Tamara's visit to the Anderson home. As she drove out to the Ridge Tamara recalled the tense telephone conversation she had with Mr. Anderson in September. *I wonder if he'll be as rude to me this time. I can't seem to get information from him.*

Tamara had to stop at the Ridge's volunteer fire department to ask for directions to the Anderson's home. Only a few streets had signs and few houses were numbered. She was well known by the volunteers at the fire station, as that was her usual stop when she was searching for a family. As it turned out, the Anderson's lived only two blocks from the fire station.

When Tamara drove up to Sarah Jane's home, she remembered having noticed this unusual structure several times. The central part of the home was an old 12′ by 60′ mobile home with a plywood addition built on the back and a camper attached to one end of the mobile home. In the front yard, Tamara saw a vicious-appearing pit bull with a severe case of mange. She recalled how so many Ridge families said they treated their mangy dogs with used motor oil. "It must be *used* motor oil to cure the disease," one man told her. The pit bull growled at Tamara, but the animal was chained to a tree.

Tamara proceeded to the Anderson's front door, which had come off its hinges and was leaning in front of the doorway; it would have to be physically moved aside to allow entrance. Mr. Anderson greeted Tamara at the door. "Oh, it's you," he said flatly. Mr. Anderson was a stocky broad-shouldered man, pale as if he never left the house. *He reminds me of Frankenstein from the old horror movie,* Tamara thought as she waited for him to move the door aside and invite her in. The children were still at school, and Tamara could talk privately with Mr. Anderson.

Inside the home, pieces and parts of old computers—monitors, keyboards and wires—were stacked everywhere. *Hmmm, when we talked on the phone, he did say he had a home-based computer business,* Tamara remembered.

Not seeing an empty spot on which to sit, she remained standing during their conversation.

Hoping to build rapport and get the ball rolling, Tamara again asked Mr. Anderson about his business. "You know, I've just gotten into using eBay for shopping recently. It's so interesting learning to shop on the computer. How long have you been in Internet sales anyway?"

"Long enough," he replied.

"And you sell . . . what was it?"

"Art and stuff."

"Art?"

But Mr. Anderson turned his back and did not reply. He had closed down again. Tamara changed the subject.

"Mr. Anderson, the school nurse has been really worried about Sarah Jane, and so am I. We know you are doing the best you can, raising your children without their mom; but we were wondering how we might assist you in helping her get healthier. Her blistered lips are really getting in the way of her learning."

Mr. Anderson sat in the one empty chair and began to type away at the keyboard.

"Yeah, she's got a case all right." He made no eye contact with Tamara.

"And, of course, we're worried about the lice in her hair as well," Tamara continued. "I know you don't want her scratching her scalp all the time and being embarrassed around the other children, do you?"

"Naw."

"I was wondering if there was any way I could help you figure out a way to get Sarah Jane well again?"

"Mebbe."

As they talked, Tamara's private thoughts continued, *He's making me a bit nervous, but I'm not sure why. I come into homes in the Ridge all the time. Why am I so nervous now?*

"It must be tough raising these three kids without their mom."

"Yep."

I'm trying to empathize, but he's not gonna open up, thought Tamara. *Best to just try and keep a foot in the door.*

"Well, Mr. Anderson, I'd like to come by and help Sarah Jane learn how to take care of her hair and her lips, if you don't mind. These problems are really getting in the way of her learning."

"Suit yourself," he muttered, as he ushered Tamara toward the door.

"I'll call you tomorrow to set up a time."

On her way out, Tamara looked with dismay at the stacks of electronic parts, the soiled blankets on the sofa, the dried food on stacks of plates. *I wonder how these kids live like this. I'd like to ask more about his computer business, but he's not letting me go there.*

SOMETHING IS JUST NOT RIGHT

As she drove away from the Anderson's home, Tamara felt sad and worried. She wanted to involve CPS to report that the Anderson kids were being neglected and she had some evidence because she had observed the lice, lack of medical care, and unsanitary home. Beyond neglect, Tamara also had a feeling that Mr. Anderson might be involved in child pornography in his Internet business and that the children might be at risk in some way. But without much evidence, the CPS workers might think that she was overreacting.

When I've had families like this before, I've made referrals to CPS. They are pretty good about following up with abuse cases, but with these neglect situations, nothing ever changes. Tamara was discouraged. *What could possibly be different this time?*

Tamara had a haunting suspicion. *Something creepy is going on here.* She had noted a stack of "men's magazines" in a corner, but there was nothing else to substantiate her suspicions about pornography that might involve the children. *I would be laughed right out of the courtroom if I have no more evidence than a stack of* Playboys, she thought. *The children never have given any indication that they have been sexually abused but clearly they fear their father. There's never been any bruises or injuries reported. But something is just not right in that home.*

I've got to do something about this, she determined. *But what? Even if they investigate for neglect, the Andersons' problems will just go on. All the families in the Ridge just seem like hopeless cases.* Tamara felt mentally exhausted as she drove out of the Ridge and back toward home where Johnny was waiting.

Case 10

If Only . . . ![1]

BARBARA HEARD MUELLER

Hospice social worker Alice Singletary was thinking about June Plunket and her family as she drove down a Louisiana highway under trees that created a leafy green tunnel. It was a beautiful day in April 2000 and the spring foliage presented a stark contrast to Alice's somber feelings. *It's not easy dealing with death everyday,* she thought. *And this is not an easy case. I have a dying woman and an angry, hysterical caregiver who hasn't accepted the approaching death of her mother. Both need help.* As a new social worker at Magnolia Hospice, Alice was still trying to "figure everything out." As she drove further away from the Plunket home and toward Magnolia Hospice she asked herself aloud, "Where do I start?"

MAGNOLIA HOSPICE

Magnolia Hospice was founded in 1982 in Alexandria, Louisiana. The colorful brochure that described the hospice noted the mission statement: "to enhance the quality of life for individuals and families dealing with life-limiting illness

---

1. This decision case was prepared solely to provide material for class discussion and not to suggest either effective or ineffective handling of the situation depicted. While based on field research regarding an actual situation, names and certain facts may have been disguised to protect confidentiality. The author and editors wish to thank the anonymous case reporter for cooperation in making this account available for the benefit of social work students and instructors. Copyright © 2005 Thomson Learning.

and assist bereaved family members by providing comprehensive, coordinated care and support." Magnolia offered "medical, emotional, and spiritual care for persons with life expectancies of six months or less."

Consistent with hospice philosophy, Magnolia offered palliative, or "comfort" care, which focused on managing pain and other symptoms, as well as grief education and counseling. The goal was to provide quality of life in the time that remained. In addition to patient care, Magnolia addressed needs of the patient's family and loved ones, providing services such as support groups and education groups facilitated by a grief counselor.

A hospice team coordinated services to patients and families, and each staff member played an important role in treating the whole person. Two physicians were in charge of patient care and ordered medicine, equipment, treatment, and other hospice services. Four nurses (RNs) made regular visits to patients and were available for emergencies, 24 hours a day, 7 days a week. Three nurse technicians helped with personal care (e.g., bathing, toileting). Three social workers, one MSW and two BSWs, offered education and counseling and linked patients to community resources, when needed. Two chaplains offered spiritual support, and a team of volunteers helped with transportation, fixing meals, relieving caregivers, and many other tasks. One of the best features of the agency was a comprehensive in-service training program in which staff members met weekly to learn about issues of death and grief. The staff members were close to one another, and were encouraged to discuss any grief in their own lives and to share openly about the emotional effects the job had on them.

FROM INTERN TO BSW SOCIAL WORKER

Alice joined the staff of Magnolia Hospice in January 2000 and had been excited to get a job immediately after graduating in December with her BSW from Northeastern University in Monroe. Her senior field internship had been with Providential Hospice of Monroe. There she had a very experienced and dedicated supervisor who taught her a great deal about practice with those who were dying and grieving. Although the work was tough, she felt competent and challenged in ways that felt good to her. As graduation came closer, Alice decided she would look for a job in hospice work. Twenty-two and single, she decided to look for a job in Alexandria, her home town, so she could be closer to her family and visit them often. When she secured the job at Magnolia, she borrowed money from her parents to pay the deposit on her first apartment and was happy to be living on her own.

Alice felt excited as she eagerly learned her way around the new job. Although many of the policies and procedures of Magnolia Hospice were similar to what she had experienced at Providential, the different personalities of the interdisciplinary team made the job unique. She enjoyed the interdisciplinary collaboration, and she was pleased that as a social worker she had a specific role on the team and special knowledge and skills. Sometimes, she felt "young" when working with nurses and physicians so much older and more experienced. They were kind and nurturing in the team meetings, and she was in awe of them. But at times she found herself intimidated by their vast experience and knowledge, and it could be difficult to confront or even make suggestions to older and more experienced team members. She was glad to have another BSW social worker, Linda Cheavons, on the team and her supervisor, Janet Sails, MSW, who was always ready to listen to her concerns and "back her up" when needed.

MEETING JUNE PLUNKET

After "shadowing" Janet for a month, Alice began taking cases on her own in February. *I want to do everything right,* she thought as she carefully read the file before visiting the Plunket home. *I need to do a good assessment of their situation and see how the team can help.* Mrs. Plunket, age 71, was dying of colon cancer. Two days before, St. Joseph's Hospital had contacted Magnolia Hospice when June was discharged. A nurse visited the family that afternoon. The nurse noted in the file that June was having significant pain, and she detailed the medication that the physician had prescribed. She also noted that the family had few resources and were concerned about payment for hospice services. *That's where a social worker can help,* Alice thought proudly to herself. The nurse had talked to Polly Quiller, June's daughter, and documented that Polly was having trouble accepting her mother's illness. Polly expressed guilt, but mostly anger toward the doctor, who had been treating June for the past four years, and had finally referred June to Magnolia Hospice. Polly blamed Dr. Dubuis for her mother's present condition. Finally, the nurse documented that the family seemed wary of strangers coming into their home.

Alice drove about 12 miles out to the Plunket home. As she opened the car door and stepped into the yard she observed that the house had peeling paint and missing window screens. The yard was cluttered with trash, plastic bottles, and aluminum cans. A path wound between the piles of debris to the house. Alice had to walk around to the back door, because a stack of cardboard boxes blocked the front door. When Polly opened the door, Alice immediately noticed the odor of illness and unwashed bodies. When Alice saw Polly, she was taken aback. Polly appeared to be about five feet four inches tall and to weigh approximately 350 pounds. She was dressed in sweatpants and a stained T-shirt. She had a pair of rubber flip-flops on her stained and dirty feet. Her hair was oily and hung below her shoulders. It appeared she had not washed it recently. She had a cup of coffee in one hand and a cigarette in the other. Her eyes were puffy, and it appeared that she had been crying.

"You must be the social worker," Polly said by way of greeting Alice. Reluctantly she said, "Come on in. Mom's in the bedroom, but she's not much of one fer company."

Alice confirmed that she was a social worker from Magnolia Hospice, and gave Polly her business card. As they stepped into the front room, Alice assured Polly she would be sensitive to her mother's condition and her feelings. "However, in order for us to give your mother the best of care and identify the things we can do to support you, it is necessary for us to talk about what is happening with both of you."

As she spoke, Alice looked around a room crowded with furniture. Old magazines and newspapers lay on the floor, tables, and the back of the sofa and stacked up in every corner. A layer of dust covered the tables, lamps, and homemade craft items such as the yarn flowers stuck in bottles, as well as the magazines and newspapers. The two windows in the room had torn shades. An oscillating fan sat on top of a pile of magazines, slowly moving back and forth. Nevertheless, the fetid odor of unwashed bodies and stale food hung over the room.

"Excuse the mess," Polly said, "but I haven't had much time to straighten up for Mom since I moved in with her. The bedroom's back this way."

As they entered the bedroom, Alice noted that it was as cluttered as the living room. June Plunket lay in the middle of a sagging double bed. Her sheets were twisted and hanging off to one side. Oxygen equipment and a potty chair sat next to the bed. Everywhere Alice looked there were dozens of Kleenex tissue flowers, crepe paper decorations, and Christmas ornaments made of bottle caps and clothespins. Wal-Mart bags full of glitter, glue, beads, pipe cleaners, crepe paper rolls, and boxes of Kleenex tissues stacked in every available space. One of the windows in June's room was boarded up to cover a broken pane.

"Hello, honey," June said weakly, "come on in and have a seat. Polly, get those magazines off that chair so this lady can sit down."

Leaning against the door, Polly explained, "Mom's pretties are everywhere. Before she got so sick, she'd spend hours making flowers and Christmas ornaments. Why, she supplied half the people in our neighborhood with flowers every year. She won't let me move or get rid of nothin'. We do get pleasure from just lookin' at them things now."

Alice walked over to the bed and squeezed June's hand, which lay limp on the bed. "Hello, Mrs. Plunket, my name is Alice."

As they talked, June lit a cigarette. Alice was alarmed when June held her cigarette close to the bed covers. In fact, she was so distracted by the cigarette that she did not hear June's next sentence. Alice looked at the oxygen canister beside the bed, which June was not using.

When June finished her sentence, Alice asked, "Mrs. Plunket, have you smoked for very long?"

"Honey, I've smoked since I was 10 years old," June replied, "and I'm not about to quit now."

"I understand," Alice replied, "but be careful when you smoke, not to catch the covers on fire."

Her face creased in pain, June began weeping softly. "I don't have much pleasure left except my cigarettes now. The pain in my gut is bad. I can't eat and I can't sleep. Can't somebody make the pain go away?"

Alice turned to Polly. "Has she had her pain medication?"

"Yeah," Polly replied, "the nurse brought it and I gave her a pain pill only a few minutes before you came."

EXPLAINING HOSPICE SERVICES

After checking on June's immediate pain, Alice began to explain the purpose of her visit. "Mrs. Plunket, you and Polly will be active participants in developing your care plan. The information you give me today and on my next visit will help our hospice team understand your needs and wishes. I'll share your information with our hospice team. You'll have choices all along the way." She went on to describe how hospice worked.

"Do I have to go to the hospital to get all these services?" June interrupted.

"No ma'am, hospice is designed to serve people in their homes," Alice said.

Alice explained that most patients prefer to be at home during this time, and that if this was her choice, nurses and nurse techs would come to the home to provide care. She also assured them that if a return to the hospital was necessary, Magnolia would assist in that transition.

"But I don't have no money to pay for all this fancy stuff," June interrupted again. "My daughter, granddaughter, and her two young'uns and me all live on my social security. I only get $850 a month. We just barely get by."

Before Alice could answer, Polly interrupted with her own question, "What do you mean about telling stuff to your team? We don't want all these folks knowing our business."

Alice explained that her mother had signed a form that would allow the members of the treatment team, which included Dr. Nelson (the hospice doctor), Alice, four nurses, three nurse techs, and a chaplain, to know about her situation so that they could suggest ways to help the two women with emotional, physical, and financial issues related to June's illness.

"Mom wouldn't be dying," Polly blurted, "if that sorry Dr. Dubuis hadn't lied to us. It's all his fault that we thought she was cured. If only I hadn't listened to him." She began crying again.

Alice offered Polly a tissue from the box sitting by June's bed and said, "I know this is very hard for you to talk about, but let me tell you what you and June may expect from our agency. Perhaps this information will give you an idea of what to expect of us." Alice went on to explain that the agency provided a continuum of care and services ranging from the development of the individual treatment plan to home visits and help with transportation, errands, and companionship. She assured them that the team was prepared to provide not only nursing care but also the kind of care offered by a good friend or neighbor.

CONDUCTING THE SOCIAL ASSESSMENT

After explaining hospice services, Alice wanted to begin the social assessment. "Mrs. Plunket, I would like to hear more about you. It helps us develop a plan that works for you when you tell us a bit about yourself."

"I've done the best I could with what I have all my life," June responded. "I got married young, too young, to a man I just didn't appreciate enough. We had two young'uns, one right after the other. Polly here was the first." June became tearful. "She has always been my sweet baby girl."

"Mom, I love you, too," Polly began to cry softly. "If only I had been a better daughter and stayed after that stupid doctor, you wouldn't be so sick."

Alice sat quietly and gave both women time to compose themselves before proceeding with the assessment.

June continued to describe her early life while Alice listened and took notes. She said her son, Billy Ray, was two years younger than Polly, "he's all grown up now and never comes around. We haven't seen him in over a year now. His dad, Roger, my first husband, lives three blocks from here and he don't have much time to visit either one of us."

"That sorry, no-count brother of mine," Polly snorted, "thinks he's too good to have anything to do with us. Him with all his education and high-paying job, and not a penny to give Mom. He knows she's having a hard time, but he don't care. Would you believe I called him after I quit my job to come live with Mom? I told him we had only the $850 and Mom's medicine was costing an arm and a leg. He told us he had too many expenses of his own and didn't have a dime to spare."

Alice asked June if she had any contact with her ex-husband, and June described an ongoing relationship with him. "He comes for birthdays and Christmas and Thanksgiving holidays." June said, "That Roger, I shoulda never left him. He's been so good to come over and visit and to help out as much as his wife will let him. He started helping a little here and there after my second husband, James Michael, died back in '92."

COURSE OF JUNE'S ILLNESS

Alice had studied the case file, which had notes from the physician and nurses, but she wanted June and Polly to describe the course of June's illness in their own words.

"We first saw Dr. Dubuis in 1996 for colon problems," Polly began. "He did all sorts of tests and took the longest to give us the news. Mom had her first surgery, a resection of her colon. After that," Polly said, "the doctor said he had gotten it all and we were cured."

"Then the cancer came back and we had another tumor removed in April 1998. This time we had chemotherapy and radiation. We were so sick, but I was still working and couldn't be with her like I should have been," Polly said, looking at her mother with affection. "Then, when was the next surgery Mom?

"In 1999," June recalled. "I believe it was in the summer, maybe July, that was another colon resection.

"Oh yeah," Polly said, "and then we were OK until this spring. I don't know the exact date, it was a couple of weeks ago, we went back to the hospital. That's when Dr. Dubuis told us that the cancer had metastasized. But what does he know? He lied to us before, telling us that Mom was cured. So, maybe he's lying now."

Her denial runs deep, Alice thought. Alice jumped in, "The file I looked at said that Wednesday, April 3, the doctor discharged June from the hospital and made the referral to us at Magnolia Hospice. Does that sound right?

"That's right," June said, "and I've been home two days, since Wednesday."

POLLY: PRIMARY CAREGIVER

Alice had been listening and taking notes. She turned to Polly, who had been doing most of the talking. "Polly, we know more about your mother now, but what about you? We'd like to hear about you, too. If you're going to be caring for your mother and working with us to ensure your mother's comfort, it would help us to develop a plan that would work for both of you if we had more information about you, as well."

"I graduated from high school in 1970, then went right to work. I had lots of jobs over the years. None of 'em ever seemed to be what I liked. I was always lookin' for something that I could do and be my own boss. Before I moved in with Mom I was manager of an RV park. That was a good job because I had my own trailer and was pretty much my own boss. But then when Mom got sick I needed to quit to move in here with Mom and take care of her."

The move left Polly with no income, no health insurance, and no unemployment insurance. They had to make June's monthly social security benefits of $850 stretch to cover all expenses. The electricity had been cut off on two different occasions because they did not have the money to pay the bill.

As they continued to talk, Alice learned that Polly was twice divorced and had a sporadic employment record. More immediately, Polly was not handling the emotions surrounding the caregiving role with her mother very well. She reported taking Xanax, but Alice observed high levels of guilt, weepiness, and anger about her mother's illness. *These emotions are typical,* Alice thought, *but I'd like to help her deal with them.*

Polly continued, "As if we didn't have enough on our mind, my daughter Jenna ups and moves in here with her two young'uns. Her good-for-nothin' husband left her for that little hussy next door to them. I told her about him before they ever got married. If he left his first wife to hook up with her, what guarantee did she have that he wouldn't do it again? And her with all her problems. You know, she's a manic-depressive and has to take medicine all the time. I just don't know what will happen to her and them kids if her husband cuts them out of his insurance. You talk about crowded. We're stacked in here tighter than them magazines stacked on the floor."

Alice asked if she might meet Polly's daughter and the children. She had heard someone on the phone in another room. There were shrieks and thumps followed by yells from the person on the phone. Polly yelled to Jenna to get off the phone and come in to meet the social worker. Jenna, short like her mother, but not quite as large, shuffled in with her two small children in tow. When introduced, Jenna said she had moved in to help care for Gram. Jenna and her children occupied the second bedroom. From where she sat, Alice glimpsed a room stacked with all their belongings. The children had to play in the small living room, which was next to their great-grandmother's bedroom. Jenna quickly excused herself and returned to talking on the phone, yelling intermittent warnings to the children: "Shut up, so you don't bother Gram!"

Polly did not complain about her daughter, but expressed frustration about their situation. They seemed a burden, not a help. No one had a job. Polly and Jenna each had a high school education but no marketable job skills. Each woman had a history of failed relationships and dependency. As she continued her assessment, Alice pondered, *They just don't seem to have much in the way of resources.*

When Alice asked Polly to describe days with her mother, she began to weep once again. "We're in so much pain, we can't be left alone. I can't trust Jenna to look after Mom even long enough for me to run to the store. She stays on the phone. I'm afraid something might happen to Mom, and she would never know it." Polly continued crying as she stood by June's bed, patting her on the shoulder, smoothing her hair, and adjusting her pillow.

After a minute, Polly resumed speaking. "We had been refusing to eat the past few days, hadn't we? I was so scared, because I knew she could starve if she did not eat something. So I cooked her some potato soup and made her favorite cornbread. When we said we wasn't hungry, I took. . . ." Polly lowered her head and spoke hesitantly, "I took the spoon and forced the food into her mouth."

"Oh my, what happened?" Alice asked, looking from Polly to June.

June was silent, but Polly said, "Well, she upchucked it all, right onto the covers. Then I sorta lost it. I was scared and felt bad about what I had done. I called the nurse from Magnolia and she came out. I calmed down some when she came. She helped me clean up and told me I should not try to make her eat if she's not hungry. So now I know."

As Polly recounted the incident, June began to cry.

Remembering this must upset her, Alice speculated.

"I guess I'm going to die," June said tearfully. "How can I leave when Polly needs me? If I die, she won't have nothin'."

Polly was crying, too. "If only I had paid more attention to Mom, this wouldn't have happened. I'm just going to go tell Dr. Dubuis what I think of him for lying to us. He ought to be sued. Mom, I'll get him if it's the last thing I do."

"Polly, one of the reasons I'm here today," Alice interjected gently, "is to help you understand your mother's illness. It's normal to feel this kind of anger when faced with the fact that someone you love is going to die. However, I'd like to help you to think of ways you can help your mother rather than spending so much energy on something you can't change."

HOW CAN I HELP YOU?

"Let's think of some positive things we can do," Alice said, trying to change the subject. "June, have you gone to church here in Alexandria?"

"I was raised a Baptist," June responded. "But, I haven't been to church in a long time."

"Would you like to have a minister or the chaplain who works with hospice come for a visit? Sometimes, patients find it comforting to visit about spiritual issues with a minister."

"Honey, I'll take what ever help I can get right now. Maybe it would be good to talk with a preacher," June responded.

"I can come and visit you and Polly regularly, too," Alice said. "Today, I'm going to go and take this information to the hospice team, as I explained to you, and I'll come back and visit you real soon, OK?"

"Yeah," June said softly, "you're a sweet girl, honey."

As Polly walked out with Alice, Alice took the opportunity to speak with her privately. "We're here for you, too, you know. Maybe when I come back you and I can talk some more about how *you* are feeling, would that be OK?"

"Sure," Polly agreed.

As she drove back to Magnolia and thought about the Plunkets, Alice felt her stress level rising. *This family could get pretty overwhelming! June deserves the best care she can get, but Polly's anger at Dr. Dubuis worries me. Plus, the whole hospice idea seems new to them and they don't have much in the way of resources. I'm not sure how to get started.*

Case 11

Finding Our Way[1]

MATTHEW SCHOBERT

"**A**s you all know, we're approaching our first program audit," announced Audrey Knerring, Refugee Employment Coordinator at Pathfinders Social Services. It was October 22, 2003, and the DHS staff had just gathered for their biweekly meeting. "DHS staff from Hennepin County will visit us next month to evaluate our program's effectiveness. They'll be reviewing our case files, client documentation, and our placement records, *especially* our placement records and employment plans."

Audrey paused for a moment, glanced around at her staff, and then continued, "Because of this, we need to discuss a topic that will be sensitive for some of us." She cleared her throat and then, after a brief pause, plunged forward, "Our RCA clients are limited to a maximum of 20 hours of schooling per week. They've got to spend *at least half* of their week's hours in job placement services. If clients spend more than 20 hours a week in school, then they are subject to sanction, which ranges from a reduction in their monthly stipend to termination from the program."

1. This decision case was prepared solely to provide material for class discussion and not to suggest either effective or ineffective handling of the situation depicted. While based on field research regarding an actual situation, names and certain facts may have been disguised to protect confidentiality. The author and editors wish to thank the anonymous case reporter for cooperation in making this account available for the benefit of social work students and instructors. Copyright © 2005 Thomson Learning.

Nathan Bierwirth jerked his head toward Audrey as she finished speaking. Then, he looked over at Madison and Basel, the other two employment counselors who worked with immigrants, refugees, and asylees in the greater Minneapolis, Minnesota, area. They also wore concerned looks. *What about Ayana?* The question flashed across Nathan's mind. *She could lose her RCA stipend. If that happens, there's no way she can pay her rent. She and her family are that close to being homeless. This could cost her everything!*

PATHFINDERS SOCIAL SERVICES

Pathfinders Social Services was a comprehensive social service provider for the greater Minneapolis, Minnesota, metropolitan area. It provided rehabilitation therapies, early childhood and family services, and employment services to more than 7,000 individuals and families per year. Pathfinders received federal, state, and foundation funding to operate these programs. More than 50 percent of Pathfinders' clients participated in employment services, making it the organization's largest department and making Pathfinders one of the largest private providers of employment services for people in the entire Twin Cities area. Because of the sheer volume and diversity of clients in employment services, Pathfinders operated several employment programs that served a broad range of people—people leaving welfare, persons with disabilities, the homeless, and immigrants, refugees, and asylum seekers, commonly called asylees. All employment service programs, regardless of the population served, were based on two principles: helping people build on their strengths and enabling people to overcome their challenges in order to build better lives for themselves and their families.

THE DHS UNIT

Nathan worked in the employment services department of Pathfinders Social Services as an employment counselor. Because the programs with which he worked were largely funded by the State of Minnesota, his unit was dubbed the Department of Human Services (DHS) Unit. He worked with two other employment counselors, Madison Legrande and Basel Mezlekia. Audrey Knerring, the refugee employment coordinator and their direct supervisor, also managed a caseload of clients. Each counselor provided a wide range of employment and social services to the approximately 30 clients on their caseload. Two other staff members, Abebe Kebbede, the intake coordinator, and Desta Salih, the training and advancement specialist, rounded out the DHS Unit.

One of the strengths of this staff was its zeal, diversity, and experience. Nathan, Madison, and Audrey were all college educated, in their mid-20s, full of energy, and deeply committed to the needs of immigrants, refugees, and asylees.

Madison held a bachelor's degree in sociology, and Audrey earned a bachelor's degree in human resource management. Nathan, therefore, was the only member of the DHS Unit with a social work degree. Although they were European Americans, their colleagues all happened to be former refugees from East Africa. Basel and Desta were refugees from Somalia and Abebe was a refugee from Ethiopia. Prior to emigrating to the United States, each attended college in his or her home country. Abebe and Basel each graduated with a degree in business. Desta, however, left Somalia before finishing college. Both had profound personal stories of their experiences as a refugee and these stories made invaluable contributions to the team's successful work with refugees, not to mention often electrifying their office atmosphere and staff meetings.

REFUGEE CASH ASSISTANCE–EMPLOYMENT SERVICES PROGRAM

The DHS Unit's entire caseload consisted of immigrants, refugees, and asylees. The DHS Unit provided services to these clients primarily through one of two programs: the Minnesota Family Investment Program (MFIP) or the Refugee Cash Assistance-Employment Services (RCA-ES). Immigrants, refugees, or asylees with dependent children received services through the MFIP while adult refugees without dependents enrolled in RCA-ES. RCA-ES was an eight-month, cash-assistance program funded by the federal government but administered by states. The eight-month period's start date began, not after enrollment in the program, but on arrival in the United States. Because of this, rarely did immigrants, refugees, or asylees ever receive the full eight months of cash assistance. Once enrolled in RCA-ES, refugees met with employment counselors for an initial intake and enrollment interview. During these sessions, which lasted between one to two hours and periodically involved the aid of an interpreter, employment counselors oriented clients to RCA-ES, conducted an individual assessment, and developed an individual client employment plan (EP) that detailed specific services provided by Pathfinders.

The individual assessment included two components: a client inventory and an employability assessment. The client inventory requested information about family composition and resources, housing, transportation, education and literacy, health and legal matters, social support, and, if applicable, child care needs. This portion of the intake and enrollment interview also asked clients to compose short- and long-term goals that were incorporated into the employability assessment and the employment plan. After completing this inventory, employment counselors conducted an employability assessment in which they collected and evaluated information about a client's employment capabilities. This information, which formed the basis for the third and final portion of the intake and enrollment interview, the employment plan, had to be completed within 30 days of the client's referral to RCA-ES. Generally, counselors completed this assessment in the initial interview. They would review a client's job skills, work experience, employment history, and education and training. Then, they would attempt to match the client's employment portfolio to jobs in the local job market. Often, however, counselors discovered that many refugees needed additional education and training, or professional certification or licensing for skilled employment. For clients who possessed a high school diploma or its equivalent and had adequate English literacy skills, employment counselors would simply inform them of the appropriate refresher courses and incorporate their participation in these courses into the employment plan.

At times, however, counselors interviewed clients who had little or no formal education or English literacy skills, two disadvantages that often prevented clients from securing any form of suitable employment. In these instances, they helped enroll clients in General Education Development (GED) or English as a Second Language (ESL) programs. These educational services, according to RCA-ES guidelines, could constitute only one-half of a client's employment plan. For the other half of their EP, clients were required to participate in a variety of employment activities, such as job-seeking skills, resume writing, and interview skills.

The employment plan was a written document that detailed specific services that Pathfinders would provide to RCA-ES participants, the requirements for their participation in the program, and the consequences for noncompliance. EPs required a minimum of 35 hours per week of RCA-ES approved activities. These activities included both employment and nonemployment services. Employment services included job-seeking skills and strategies, job placement, job training, and job retention. Nonemployment services referred to services such as remedial and general education, English literacy education, housing and transportation needs, health or legal services, and basic family services. The EP, like the employability assessment, had to be completed within 30 days of the client's referral to the program.

Employment counselors often found it difficult, if not impossible, to introduce and orient clients to the Refugee Cash Assistance–Employment Services program, complete two separate assessments, and develop an employment plan in the initial intake and enrollment interview. This was particularly true in those instances when clients had little or no English literacy skills and the entire process required an interpreter. Therefore, it was not uncommon for some portion of the initial interview, particularly the EP, to be carried over into the second, and at times the third, session with clients.

NATHAN BIERWIRTH, BSW

Nathan joined Pathfinders Social Services in December 2001, after graduating from Goshen College with a bachelor of science degree in social work. Although this was his first professional job, Nathan began working, as a volunteer, with refugees and their families while in college.

Nathan enrolled in Goshen College, a small, liberal arts, Christian college rooted in the Anabaptist-Mennonite peace tradition and located in Goshen, Indiana. Even as a freshman, Nathan possessed a keen vocational vision. Throughout high school he had invested his time and energy in a broad range of social service volunteer activities. He worked with a local Head Start program, tutored economically disadvantaged children in after-school programs, served food to the homeless in soup kitchens, and worked as a counselor at a summer peace camp for youth. But two of his experiences as a high school student were particularly formative for him—participating in community service trips to Native North American Indian reservations and renovating housing in economically disadvantaged neighborhoods in his hometown of Gary, Indiana.

Nathan's community service trips to a Navajo reservation in Arizona and a Crow reservation in South Dakota aroused in him a passion for cross-cultural work. And his participation in urban housing renovation projects deeply impressed on him the importance of affordable and safe housing for people struggling with poverty and homelessness. In college he found ample opportunities, through a local Habitat for Humanity chapter and a local refugee resettlement program, to pursue these two interests. But it was in his work with refugees that he discovered his true passion.

Nathan first encountered refugee issues through participation in Students for Religious Freedom (SRF), a campus organization at Goshen College. SRF promoted religious freedom and rights for persecuted minorities through community education and advocacy. At the time, Sudan was prominently in the news because of religious and ethnic violence between the Muslim majority in the north and the Christian minority in the south. The conflict displaced large numbers of people from their homes. Many displaced people sought refuge in neighboring countries and applied for refugee status to other nations, including the United States.

Once granted refugee status to the United States, resettlement agencies assisted refugees in locating housing, employment, education, and other appropriate social services. According to the U.S. Conference of Catholic Bishops, nearly one-fourth of all refugees admitted to the United States each year were resettled by Catholic Charities' refugee resettlement programs. In and around South Bend, Indiana, Catholic Charities helped resettle a number of Sudanese families. South Bend was approximately 45 minutes from Goshen and Nathan decided to get involved in volunteer work with these families. At first he participated in after-school tutoring programs for children and youth. But tutoring was only the beginning. As he learned of the immense challenges that refugees faced during resettlement, and how difficult it was for many of them to adjust to life in the United States, he was compelled to get more involved. Soon he was helping families and sponsors, usually lay people in local Catholic parishes, to recognize and advocate for community services for refugee families. Because his experiences working with Sudanese families and their sponsors were so rewarding, after graduation Nathan sought a social work job with refugees. He eagerly accepted a position at Pathfinders Social Services as an employment counselor. Nineteen months later Nathan met Ibsaa and Ayana.

IBSAA AND AYANA TUMA

"Hey, Nathan, I have two new clients for you," Abebe's heavily accented voice drifted into Nathan's office. "A brother and sister, newly arrived from Ethiopia."

"Okay, great," Nathan replied. "I'll be ready in just a minute. Just let me finish these case notes."

"Nathan," Abebe continued, "the brother speaks English, but the sister doesn't, she doesn't know any English, actually. They speak Oromo, one of the major Ethiopian languages. I know Oromo, but I can't translate for you right now. I'm sorry, but they've got two other brothers who are here, and I need to enroll them in RCA. Besides, I think the brother's English, his name is Ibsaa, is satisfactory and he can interpret for you with his sister, Ayana. He's also fairly educated and is somewhat knowledgeable about American society. That okay?"

"Sure, Abebe. That's fine. I'm sure we'll manage."

A moment later Abebe ushered the two siblings into Nathan's office. Ibsaa was dressed in typical, but conservative, Western clothes, blue jeans and a plain, short-sleeved shirt, but Ayana wore traditional Muslim garb, accentuated by a flowing hijab that wrapped around her head and left only her face, from chin to forehead, exposed. Her hijab caught Nathan's attention, but it didn't surprise him. Three of his coworkers were from eastern Africa and he had worked with numerous Muslim clients. Ibsaa and Ayana were rather short and thin; Nathan estimated that Ibsaa was perhaps 5'7" and that Ayana was at least three or four inches shorter. They were also quite young; in their early 20s, he guessed, and they had very dark complexions.

"Hi, my name is Nathan Bierwirth." Nathan smiled and offered his hand to Ibsaa, who shook it assertively. Nathan simply smiled and nodded to Ayana. "I'll be your employment counselor."

"I am Ibsaa Tuma and this is my younger sister, Ayana."

"Nice to meet you, here, have a seat. Abebe says he enrolled you in the Refugee Cash Assistance program, what we call RCA, and that he gave you some information about it. I want to explain the program to you a little more and then we need to complete some other paperwork. If we have time this afternoon, I'd like to begin developing an employment plan for you, too. Employment plans describe how we will help you to find a job. However, we probably will not get that far today."

"Abebe told me you will find us jobs," Ibsaa offered bluntly.

"That's true, Ibsaa. That's part of my . . . well, that's actually the main thing I will help you do. But to get to that point I've got to create a case file for each of you so that I can match you to a good job. Does that make sense?"

"Yes, it makes sense. Let's begin." Again, Ibsaa addressed Nathan in a clipped, direct fashion. Nathan wasn't sure what to make of this, but he decided to follow Ibsaa's direction at this point in the interview.

"Let's begin with the family inventory. Since you two are siblings this information will probably be the same for both of you. Ibsaa, since you know English and Ayana does not, I'll need your help for this part of the interview. Okay?"

"Yes. I will answer your questions."

Several minutes later Nathan had completed the family inventory. Despite Ibsaa's brief responses regardless of the question, Nathan learned a great deal about the Tuma family and his two new clients. Ibsaa and Ayana were only 18 months apart in age, Ibsaa was 21 and Ayana was 20. They had eight other brothers and sisters, two older brothers who were twins, and six children younger than Ayana. Because of civil unrest during 2003, the entire family, including their parents, fled from Ethiopia into Kenya. Their life in a Kenyan refugee camp was difficult, and they lived in squalor with thousands of other refugees, mostly from Ethiopia and Somalia. Finally, their application for resettlement to the United States was accepted and in July 2003 they arrived in the United States. Through Hennepin County, the State of Minnesota resettled the family in Minneapolis and referred them to Pathfinders Social Services. That day, September 12, was their enrollment date for Minnesota's Refugee Cash Assistance–Employment Services program.

Ibsaa completed high school in Ethiopia and even attended college for two years before fleeing the country, but Ayana never received formal education of any kind and had no work experience outside the home.

After completing the family inventory, Nathan went through the employability assessment with Ibsaa. Ibsaa didn't have much work experience, but he was highly motivated. That was a plus. But Ibsaa made clear a number of things during the assessment that would complicate finding employment. First, Ibsaa refused to do "woman's work." Cooking, cleaning, and child care were not acceptable employment options for him. Second, he made it clear to Nathan that he and Ayana were devout Muslims and would not work with alcohol or pork. Nathan respected their religious practices, but knew that this pretty much ruled out work at restaurants for either of them.

"Ibsaa," Nathan continued, "now that we've completed your employability assessment, would you help me go through this with your sister? Some of these questions will be the same for her, but there are others that I need to ask her. For example, did she have a job in Ethiopia?"

"No, she did not. She never worked outside the home."

"I understand. What type of work-related tasks did she do at home?

"She is the oldest daughter. She and our mother did all the cooking and cleaning. They took care of the young children and the home. That is it. That is all that was expected."

"Ibsaa, can you ask Ayana what kind of jobs she would like to do here in the States?"

Without hesitation Ibsaa replied, "She can do cleaning."

"Could you ask her? I'd really like to know what she thinks."

Ibsaa turned and spoke to Ayana. It was quiet in Nathan's office for a moment and then Ayana spoke in a very soft voice.

"She does not know what kind of work there is for her to do, but she can do cleaning. That is what she did in Ethiopia. That is what she can do here. Cleaning, cooking, or taking care of children."

"Ayana," Nathan politely addressed his next question to her, "when would you like to work? In the mornings, afternoons, or evenings?"

Ibsaa gazed at Nathan and then spoke to his sister. Again, she was quiet for a moment and then made a short reply. "Afternoons," announced Ibsaa. "She has duties at home to do in the mornings and evenings."

"What about school, Ayana? It will be important for you to learn English. Are you willing to go to school?"

When Ibsaa translated these questions, Nathan noticed that Ayana's head raised ever so slightly. "Yes," Ibsaa said, "she would like to learn English. Learning English is important. She must do this."

"Well, there are several options, Ibsaa. I can help you find schools that teach English. We call them English as a Second Language schools, or ESL for short. There are many ESL programs in the city. They are all similar, but you will want to visit many of them in order to find the best fit for Ayana. There are even classes you can take to improve your English." Nathan discussed ESL options for a few more minutes with Ibsaa and then noticed how late in the afternoon it was. They had been working on the initial intake forms for nearly two hours, and, as he had suspected, they had only completed the family inventory and the job placement survey. They had not even begun the employment plan. *No problem,* he thought, *we've got 30 days to complete the EP.*

"We're almost out of time this afternoon," Nathan remarked. "Pathfinders offers employment classes that you need to attend as part of your participation in the RCA program. The classes meet every Tuesday and Thursday morning from 9:00 to 10:30. The classes teach basic job-seeking skills that will be very important in helping you find work. How about the three of us meet on Thursdays right after class, from 10:30 to 11:30? Since Abebe is usually busy during that time, Ibsaa, it will be very helpful if we all meet together so you can translate for Ayana. Does this sound alright with you?"

Ibsaa spoke to Ayana and then agreed with Nathan's proposal. As they left his office, Nathan's mind began to race as he thought about the challenges he anticipated working with Ibsaa and Ayana. *He's motivated, has some education, and can speak English. I bet we can find him a job. But Ayana,* Nathan shook his head, *it's gonna be hard to find work for her, especially since she can't even communicate in English at all. That's gotta be our first priority, getting her plugged into some ESL classes. Then we can go from there.*

AN ALTERNATIVE PLAN

The next Thursday, Ibsaa and Ayana showed up for their first employment services class, but 10 minutes into the class Ibsaa left saying he had a doctor's appointment. Abebe was busy enrolling clients after the class and without anyone to translate for Ayana, there was nothing to be gained by meeting, so Ayana took the bus home.

Ibsaa showed up for their meeting the following Thursday, but without Ayana. "Ayana is sick," he informed Nathan. He also told Nathan that she had enrolled in an ESL program that would begin the first of October. At first Nathan was elated. *Finally,* he thought, *some good news for Ayana. This is exactly what she needs.*

But then Ibsaa continued, "Ayana cannot come to our appointments anymore. Her classes begin at 9:45 in the morning and end at 4:30. She is at school all day."

"Does she go to school every day of the week?" Nathan asked.

"Yes. She is in school all week. I do not need as many English classes as she does, so I can still come to see you for both of us."

"Well, Ibsaa, it's important for me to meet with Ayana, too, although I'm not sure how this will work with her being in class all day. Perhaps I can arrange to do phone contacts with her in the mornings before she leaves for class. Do you think that will work?"

Ibsaa explained that the entire family lived in two apartments, but shared one phone line. The phone was in Ibsaa's apartment, which he shared with several brothers. Ayana lived with their parents and the younger children in a nearby apartment. But for the time being, this seemed the best plan under the circumstances. Nathan would talk to Ayana over the phone, with the help of Ibsaa or one of her other brothers who spoke English, and Ibsaa would serve as a "go-between" of sorts for Nathan as well. This was far from the ideal arrangement, but Ayana's lack of English literacy required someone's help in communicating with her and she certainly needed the maximum amount of English language training that she could get at this point. In a couple of months, Nathan surmised, Ayana would be able to communicate with him on a basic level and then they could begin to work together more directly. Plus, by that time, she would be able to get something out of Pathfinders' employment services classes, too. *I think this might work,* he thought.

WEDNESDAY MORNING'S UNIT MEETING

Nathan settled himself into one of the chairs around the conference room table. As his fellow DHS staff arrived for their biweekly meeting his thoughts drifted to Ayana. *I'm starting to feel frustrated,* he admitted to himself. *I've tried to call her several times the past few weeks, but nobody ever answers the phone. Ibsaa tells me she's doing fine and making a lot of progress in her English classes, but I would really like to speak with her myself.* In spite of this, Nathan believed Ayana's case was going about as well as could be expected. Audrey's voice interrupted his thoughts and he turned his attention to her as the meeting started.

"As you all know, we're approaching our first program audit," she announced. "DHS staff from Hennepin County will visit us next month to evaluate our program's effectiveness. They'll be reviewing our case files, client documentation, and our placement records, *especially* our placement records and employment plans. So, I thought we should use today's meeting to review exactly how these records should be prepared. I'm not worried about case files for our MFIP clients. We've got plenty of experience with the Minnesota Family Investment Program and I know our case files are all correctly documented. Since June, however, we've started enrolling clients in the new Refugee Cash Assistance program through the state. Although there are a lot of similarities between RCA and MFIP, there are a number of important differences. So, since we're operating under some new rules and policies, I want everyone to be clear on the differences in documentation for RCA clients so that our audit goes smoothly."

"For the most part there's not much difference in reporting or documentation. However," she cleared her throat and then, after a brief pause, plunged forward, "the new rules limit our client's hours for schooling. If you recall Hennepin County's RCA training session back in May, RCA clients are limited to a maximum of 20 hours of schooling per week, and they've got to spend *at least* half of their week's hours in job placement services. If clients spend more than 20 hours a week in school then they are subject to sanction, which ranges from a reduction in their monthly stipend to termination from the program."

Nathan quickly craned his head to get a good look at Audrey, and then he turned to gauge Madison's and Basel's response to this information. They too wore concerned looks. *What about Ayana?* The question flashed across Nathan's mind. *She could lose her RCA stipend. If that happens, there's no way she can pay her rent. She and her family are that close to being homeless. This could cost her everything!* In light of Audrey's comments about restrictions for RCA clients, Ayana's case suddenly seemed desperate.

"Just how serious are these sanctions?" Basel asked. "I mean, how seriously will Hennepin County be in enforcing sanctions?"

"They will enforce the RCA policies very strictly," Audrey responded. "I know, I can tell you from personal experience."

"Personal experience?" ventured Madison gingerly.

"Back in June I had an RCA client who was enrolled in school for 32.5 hours a week. She had very little education and only knew a little English. She needed to be in school, so I called the RCA administrator at Hennepin County to see if this was acceptable or not and the administrator told me my client was exceeding the maximum amount of schooling hours per week allowed by RCA."

"What happened?" Madison asked. "Did they sanction her or anything?"

"The Hennepin County RCA administrator turned out to be a real stickler for following and enforcing the rules. My client," Audrey replied, "she lost all of her RCA assistance."

Madison gasped, "Everything!" The other staff clearly shared her shock as everyone started talking at once.

Finally, Abebe's voice won out, "What did you do? Were you able to do anything?"

"Yes, I was able to switch her to a general assistance program. Its monthly stipend was much lower than the RCA stipend, but it was something and it was the best I could do."

"General assistance, Audrey?" Madison asked. "Those payments aren't much. I mean, RCA stipends aren't much either, but they sure beat GAs. How could she make it on just GA?"

"It was incredibly difficult, you almost can't imagine what that did to her, and it caused me a lot of grief, too. Believe me. I felt responsible, and even a little guilty. But what else could I do?"

"So what you're saying," Nathan began, "is that any of our clients who are in school more than part time are in clear violation of the RCA guidelines and the consequence is that they get terminated from the program?"

"That's right. Now, I know we've only got a few clients that this applies to, but nonetheless, this is a real dilemma we've got to face regarding reporting to DHS and we need to decide how we're going to deal with it. The long and short of it is we need to decide how we will report schooling hours for these clients."

"I'm just curious," asked Madison, "just how many clients are we talking about here? I only have one RCA client who needs to be in school more than part time."

"Right now I have two clients," answered Audrey.

"I also have two clients," Basel added.

"So, according to the RCA rules," Nathan interjected again, "clients like Ayana, who is my only client who has no English literacy skills, can only be in ESL for 20 hours a week and they've got to be in employment services for the other 20? What good will employment service programs do if they can't understand what's being said?"

"I know, I know," Audrey responded, "but that's what it comes down to."

"Audrey, Ayana only receives $250 in support each month from RCA. She gets $150 in cash and $100 in food stamps. It takes her *and* her parents *and* her siblings pooling all their cash payments to cover their rent and living expenses. Food stamps cover the bulk of their food costs and we provide them with city bus passes for transportation. They don't have much money to work with. They, and I'm sure most of the other RCA clients, are on *tight* budgets. If she loses her $250, there is no way that family of 10 can manage to afford two apartments, not to mention feed everyone."

"You see, you see. You cannot report these clients," Abebe implored, vigorously jumping into the conversation. "Nathan is right, he's right. How can they make it? They must learn English first. They just must! How else can they find a job? I know how important schooling is for clients who don't know English. I know what it's like to be a refugee in America. It is not easy, and I even knew some English when I arrived. But Ayana and others like her, they do not know any English. They need to learn English; they need to learn about American culture, they need to know these things before they can get a job. The rules are wrong. The rules are wrong. Audrey, you cannot report these clients."

Desta didn't say anything, but her grim expression and a nod of the head signaled her agreement with Abebe. As a former refugee, she too knew how precarious life was for refugees and how invaluable English literacy was for any hopes of landing a job and making it in society.

"Abebe, I hear you. I know what you're saying is pretty accurate. If it makes you feel any better, I'm not going to report my clients for exceeding their classroom hours."

"You're not?" Basel stammered, a look of surprise blanketing his face.

"No, in fact, I spoke to my supervisor about this immediately after my first RCA client was sanctioned. Caitlin was sympathetic and didn't see the sense in the part-time limitation for clients with no English literacy skills. We discussed it and as far as she and the other supervisors over our department are concerned, it's up to us as to how we want to report this. So, I guess I want to know what you guys think. Are you okay with reporting it this way for clients with no English literacy or can you think of some other way for us to handle this problem?"

Audrey surveyed her staff. It was clear what Abebe and Desta thought, but since they were not employment counselors, this was not their decision.

Madison spoke first, "Well, if this is okay with you, Audrey, and if it's okay with Caitlin, since you're the supervisors then I don't have any qualms about fudging the schooling hours for my RCA client."

"But what happens if Hennepin County discovers we falsely reported on a client's employment plan?" Nathan questioned. "Isn't that fraud?"

"I see this first and foremost as a matter of seeking what's best for our clients. I think that is our primary goal. But, you're probably right, Nathan. This could be taken as welfare fraud. Which means, I'm sure," Audrey continued, "that we run the risk of losing our RCA funding."

"And with no RCA funding we'll lose all our RCA clients," Basel muttered.

"Yes, that's the risk," Audrey confirmed. "But, since the number of our clients in need of full-time ESL is so small, a total of six out of our combined caseloads, it's not much of a risk. The audit will be a random sampling of all of our case files, and unless the auditors make the unusual decision to initiate a thorough investigation of our files, which is unheard of unless files are incomplete, documentation is excessively sloppy, or there's some reason to believe files are inaccurate, or an agency has a history of compliance problems, then nothing will happen. And remember, these clients only receive eight months of RCA money to begin with, and that's if they're lucky enough to be enrolled immediately after arriving in the United States. The way RCA is set up, none of them will be long-term cases. Because they have such a short amount of time to get settled, and because their needs are so great during the initial stages of resettlement, I think it's ethically justifiable to make sure our non-English speaking clients are afforded the best opportunity possible for making it that we can give them. And that may mean that these six clients need to be attending ESL full time. Nathan, Basel, you do not have to go along with my decision, it is mine and mine alone, so please don't feel pressure from me. I just want you to know where I stand and what I intend to do."

Basel managed to make eye contact with Nathan and Nathan knew why. Nathan imagined that Basel was sympathetic to the needs of these clients, much like Abebe and Desta. However, Basel was also a practicing Muslim, and Nathan knew that he took the ethical obligations of his Islamic faith extremely seriously. He was one of the most ethical people Nathan had ever worked with, and Nathan could imagine the struggle raging within Basel— whether to do what he genuinely believed was in the best interests of his two clients and falsely report their education hours or to accurately report their hours knowing they would be terminated from the program and lose their financial assistance. Basel had asked Nathan for counsel on ethical dilemmas in the past, and Nathan figured Basel was waiting to see what he did this time. Even though Nathan was Christian, Basel respected his opinion. In a peculiar sense, both men trusted one another's judgment precisely because of their sincere faith commitments. And yet Nathan grew increasingly uncomfortable at the thought that Basel might follow his example. *Making my own decision on this is hard enough,* he thought, *but knowing Basel is watching and waiting to decide based on what I say makes this even more complicated.*

Case 12

In Her Best Interest[1]

DUNCAN T. WHYTE

On a warm, humid April morning in 1998, Debra Masters walked out of her office and down the hall to the bathroom in a renovated historical home in Charleston, South Carolina. *I had been looking forward to working with Stephanie,* Debra thought as she wiped a drop of sweat from her forehead. *Why am I so anxious now? I was sure she would be the ideal client—verbal, intelligent, what was that acronym from graduate school? YAVIS—young, attractive, verbal, intelligent, and successful. I've never had to walk out of an interview before, but I can't seem to focus. I wonder if Stephanie can tell that I'm distracted?*

DEBRA MASTERS

Debra Masters was raised as a traditional Caucasian Southern woman in a home that she described to her colleagues as "very conservative, fundamentalist Baptist." At 15, she started dating the man she would eventually marry. After they married at 21, she began working on her bachelor's degree at a state university.

1. This decision case was prepared solely to provide material for class discussion and not to suggest either effective or ineffective handling of the situation depicted. While based on field research regarding an actual situation, names and certain facts may have been disguised to protect confidentiality. The author and editors wish to thank the anonymous case reporter for cooperation in making this account available for the benefit of social work students and instructors. Copyright © 2005 Thomson Learning.

It was during a popular "Sexuality 101" college course, however, that she began to develop an awareness of her potential as a lesbian or bisexual woman. "I dare say," Debra later shared with a colleague, "I had no understanding of the possibility of a sexual love relationship between two women. I had lived a very sheltered life up to then. I had no template for conceptualizing gay relationships. I had these feelings for other women, but I thought everyone felt like I did and that it was normal. Anyway, I was married and it seemed irrelevant at that point."

After graduating from college Debra worked as a health educator for about 10 years, first at a mental health clinic and then a women's health clinic. In these positions she provided health promotion services such as adolescent health, sex education, and substance abuse prevention. Debra then entered graduate school with the goal of developing clinical mental health skills.

She had had an interesting social work career since earning her MSW. First, she provided a wide range of counseling services at New Directions, a counseling center associated with a Methodist church, where she had an advanced year field placement. Her field supervisor and the director of the center, Dan Corley, hired her after graduation and the two became close professional colleagues. Within four years, Debra also started a part-time private practice.

While working at New Directions it became increasingly clear that Debra's marriage had begun to flounder. Her husband, who was a 40-year-old highly educated professional, was seemingly in the midst of a fairly traditional mid-life crisis. After being turned down for a major promotion he announced to Debra that he no longer wanted to be married, and they subsequently divorced. After some long thought and reflection, Debra realized that her identity as a person was no longer going to be defined by her marriage. She then cautiously and discreetly began dating other women. "I didn't know where it would lead," she said, "but for the first time in many years I felt free to let things happen as they were going to happen."

NEW DIRECTIONS FOR DEBRA

After her divorce, Debra became more and more comfortable in relationships with women, identifying herself as bisexual more than homosexual. As her confidence and comfort in this role grew, her professional relationship with Dan Corley at New Directions became more trusting as well. Finally, she decided to tell him of her new relationship with a woman. Debra fondly recalled her relationship with Dan. "He had been there through the breakup with my husband and my divorce. I wanted to be who I was, where I was. He was always very supportive and was not a prejudiced person. I was not hiding as much any more. I wanted to share my joy with him, that I was happy again and that I was loving again."

When Debra told Dan of her sexual orientation and new relationship, Dan went ashen. Dan was silent, then said, "The Methodist church has a 'don't ask–don't tell' policy, Debra. You've put me in a position where I have to make a decision."

Debra didn't think it was fair to place that burden on Dan so she resigned. After a six-year professional relationship with him, the parting was especially sad for Debra. She had begun to realize some of the costs of her decision to disclose.

PRIVATE PRACTICE

After leaving New Directions, Debra continued her part-time private practice but also found a new job as a community organizer and life skills education coordinator with a faith-based family service organization that provided support for those transitioning to independent living. While enjoying the new job, Debra poured growing energy into the group practice with three other therapists—a licensed social worker and two licensed marriage and family therapists. Collectively they provided a variety of services including individual therapy, play therapy, couples therapy, family therapy, experiential group therapy, and spiritual direction. During this time she became increasingly "out," both personally and professionally, starting with colleagues in her private practice. One of her colleagues received a significant number of referrals from churches and faith-based organizations for play therapy and couples therapy. Debra realized it would not be fair to her colleagues or to her colleagues' clients if they found out about Debra's sexual orientation from others. Debra reasoned that she needed to let her colleagues make an informed decision about the potential impact of her sexual orientation on their practice. To her great relief, she found her colleagues to be very accepting and inclusive.

THE INITIAL INTERVIEW

After her disclosure to Dan Corley, Debra felt very apprehensive about disclosing her sexual orientation to anyone else, especially other professionals. But with the validation of her private practice colleagues, she felt a greater sense of integrity in her life, no longer having to give so much energy to keeping a secret or wondering who knew or suspected what about her. Though still working full time in the family service organization, Debra particularly looked forward to seeing her private practice clients as it was in this setting she felt she could best use the skills she had developed.

On the morning of her first appointment with Stephanie Railsback, Debra went to the office, sat down in her comfortable Shaker-style chair, looked at her planner, and noted that she was to see Stephanie at 10:00. Debra thought how refreshing it would be to engage with a client who could be insightful and reflective and who could communicate that to the therapist. Even before the session began, Debra envisioned her work with Stephanie to be some of her best therapy ever.

After the initial introductions, Debra began the session with Stephanie by asking, "What brings you to therapy now?" Stephanie was 27 years old, thin, and might be described as "femme."

Stephanie replied, "I guess I have some relationship issues to sort out—and maybe some decisions to make."

"So tell me, what's going on in your relationship that has you concerned now?" Debra inquired.

Stephanie hesitated, apparently deciding how much to tell. After a deep breath she started, "I recently broke up with a woman I really loved. I just don't think I'm ready to be in a committed relationship with a woman. I'm not really sure if I'm gay, and honestly, I'd rather be able to be with a man."

"So you're not entirely clear about your sexual orientation," Debra responded, "but practically, you think being in a committed relationship with a man would work out better for you."

"I think so," Stephanie said. "I'm just not sure. I've been in therapy before—for quite a while after I was sexually abused by my uncle. With all of these issues I still have, I wonder if I still don't have some things unfinished from that abuse. I think I still have some work to do. I'm just trying to sort a lot of things out."

"OK. Well I am glad you came in," Debra said. "Before we go any further, I usually try to tell people a little about myself and about my practice so we can see if we have a good fit, and if you are comfortable. I want clients to know who they're hiring up front so later on they don't feel they're with the wrong therapist."

"That sounds OK," Stephanie replied.

Debra continued, "I describe myself as an experiential therapist—I tend to focus on what is going on here and now in sessions. I believe a lot of conflicts for people involve developmental issues and developmental blocks."

Stephanie seemed to be listening intently, but looked puzzled about what Debra was saying.

"What I often do in therapy," Debra continued, "is offer the client speculative hypotheses or 'guesses' as vehicles to facilitate therapeutic progress. The client then reflects on these 'guesses' and lets me know how accurate they are—or are not, as the case may be. I wonder if that sounds like an approach that will be helpful for what you want to accomplish in therapy?"

Stephanie raised her eyes to the ceiling, seeming to scan her thoughts, then said, "What I'm looking for is someone to help me think and talk this through so I can come to terms with this. What you described sounds like what I had in mind."

Debra then gave Stephanie a client paperwork packet to complete at home rather than spending time at the office completing it that day. Debra then turned the interview to learning more about Stephanie's history.

Stephanie began describing her history, "I was raised by conservative parents who had been very active in their Presbyterian church. I'm still active in that church community and spirituality is a very important part of my life. I also get a lot of support from friends and my family." Debra consciously used all of the attending skills she could to encourage Stephanie's sharing. *She's really talking freely and seems very open,* Debra thought. *We'll need to focus on some of the issues she brought up at the start of the session about sexuality and relationships, because that is why she is here.*

Debra launched a question, "Tell me about your history of sexual attractions."

Stephanie spoke quietly and slowly. "I first realized I was attracted to women at an early age. I don't have a personal problem with homosexuality. As I mentioned, I recently fell very much in love with a woman. But, I just don't think I can live out a homosexual life. It's just too hard—on everybody and everything.

"It's been tough on you," Debra said in her most empathetic tone.

"Yeah," Stephanie continued. "Like for example, my parents and the members of my church would never accept me as a lesbian. It would probably kill them to find that out."

At this point Stephanie's words struck a chord with Debra. *This is starting to sound very familiar,* she thought. Debra began to remember herself struggling with those very same questions and issues and the feelings that came with them. She continued to attend to Stephanie, but she heard her own internal processing more loudly now. *Did she come to me for therapy because she knows I'm gay? Does she even know about my sexual orientation?*

As Stephanie continued she related that she really preferred a heterosexual life, but wondered whether her attraction to women would prevent that from being successful. She had at one point been engaged to a man, who eventually confronted her about her physical and emotional distance from him. He told her he suspected she was a lesbian and that, although he loved her a great deal, he couldn't continue the relationship.

As Stephanie talked, more questions started flashing in Debra's mind. *What's in her best interest here? Maybe I need to tell her I am gay—what if she finds out anyway? After all, our network of helping professionals is not large. Would she feel betrayed if she finds out about me from somebody else? And if I do tell her, when would be the best time? We haven't even developed much of a rapport yet. What if she would rather have a "straight" therapist?* As she became increasingly distracted by her own thoughts, Debra worried that she might not be fully present for her client. She wondered what she "owed" her client in terms of truthfulness and full disclosure.

As her mind flooded with questions, Debra said to herself, *The professional community is so small here, she's probably going to find out at some point from somebody that I'm lesbian.* The more she tried to work out what to do next in the room, the more anxious she became. Debra felt tremendous pressure to do the right thing.

Why am I so anxious? I'm not worried about being "out" to this woman; I just don't want to seem anxious about being "out" to her—that's something else. And if I do the wrong thing now, it could not only harm the client but also impact my professional reputation.

Wanting to interrupt her mounting anxiety, Debra took a deep breath and said to Stephanie, "I need to let you know that I am feeling anxious here and I need to take a break to make sure I'm clear about what's going on in my head. I think what happens next in our session is critical so I'd like to take a time-out to reflect on that. Is that OK?"

"Sure," she said cautiously, with a puzzled expression on her face, "that sounds OK."

Leaving the room, Debra headed for the bathroom to reflect on what she should do next.